RESTORATION

DOROTHY D. WARD

DFG PUBLISHING
Since 2014

All Scripture unless otherwise indicated, are taken from The Holy Bible, *New International Version*® NIV®. Copyright © 1973, 1978, 1984, 2001 by Biblica, Inc. ™ Used by Permission. All rights reserved worldwide.

Cover design by Tanya M. Codispodi
Interior Designer/Book Consultant: Shalena "Diva" Broaster

RESTORATION

Dedication

This book is dedicated to memory of Kevin D. Catwell.

Our countless conversations about the contents of this book over time helped me tremendously. Your profound words of encouragement helped me to realize this book has the potential to bring healing to many. Thank you for the love and support on this project while in the earthly realm. I miss you dearly, but I am certain you'd be proud!

Acknowledgments

I give honor and thanks to my Lord Jesus Christ for without you I am nothing. God, I thank you for the gifts you've bestowed upon me and for providing me with the opportunity to share them with the world. Samuel 15:22 (NIV) reads: "To obey is better than sacrifice…" Thank you for being patient with me while I attempted to do everything except obey the call to complete this literary work. I know beyond a shadow of a doubt that I am merely a messenger. Every word in this book is in alignment with my divine assignment from you. Thank you for trusting me enough to speak to your people through this book.

Dad: Thank you for just being YOU. You are such an amazing example of authenticity! You've set an unprecedented example of work ethic. My world is such a better place because you are in it. Thank you for your unconditional love and unwavering support. You are my father, but as an adult you've also been a friend, and counselor. In your presence I can bask in a judgment free zone, full of love and positive energy. Thank you for that gift. It's priceless.

Lakashia: I am truly blessed to have a sister, friend, mother, counselor, financial advisor, protector all wrapped up in one. You've made countless sacrifices as the "first born". Thank you for going ahead of me to make my path a little easier. You have such a quiet strength that I truly admire. Thank you for always supporting me and making me feel as though I can do anything. It means everything to me! I love you!

Louis: Brother, you are wise beyond your years. You are an incredibly strong, thought leader with a brilliant mind. Thank you for being unapologetic about who you are and what you stand for. I couldn't be any more proud of the man you've become. No excuses, just hard work and determination to leave a legacy of empowerment. Although younger, I have indeed learned so very much from you. I love you!

Neisha: You are a beautiful soul and I am blessed to have you in my life dear cousin. You are an amazing example of perseverance and determination. Continue to push yourself to heights unknown! I love you!

Tyron: Over the years, you've truly been an inspiration to me. I am proud to call you friend. I have never before witnessed someone so incredibly driven and passionate about their craft. You embody the tenacity required for goal attainment no matter how challenging the journey. Wishing you continued success!

My "besties" (Jessica, Lauren, Nicole, Rashed): While each of you have such incredibly different personalities and fill different spaces in my heart, you all share in the commonality of being the best friends a girl could ever have. Thank you for the most amazing 16+ years of friendship and unwavering support. You have each been there for me through all of life's trials and triumphs. Loyalty is everything and I'm so glad we all share the same definition of the word. Thank you!

Goddaughter Jordyn: Time is flying and you are almost a teenager. The world is your oyster baby girl! With hard work, diligence, and dedication there is nothing you cannot accomplish. My wish for you is that all the days of your life you will know who you are, and *whose* you are. May God order your footsteps and lead you. No matter where you are in the world, I am always here for you! I love you dearly.

To the memories of my mother and grandmother: Deborah Jean Chisolm/Dorothy Eloise Chisolm: I thank both of you guardian angels for LIFE! Without either of you I would not be who I am today and that far extends the physical. My foundation of servitude comes from each of you and I am forever grateful.

Grandma: I thank God for time I had so sit at your feet and learn what it was to pray fervent, heaven-shaking prayers. From you I learned who God was the power of prayer. You have given me one of the greatest gifts I could ever receive.

Mom: I've learned incredibly valuable lessons from you. Your life has in many ways served as my classroom. You made mistakes so I wouldn't have to—and my heart is filled with utmost gratitude. I thank you for the gift of life that I do not take for granted. I strive each day to make you proud beyond measure.

Family: For me there has always been a distinct difference between relatives and family. To each of my family members who have consistently shown me love and unwavering support—this is for you! We may or may not be related by blood, but you have earned your place in my heart over time by sharing in my highest highs and lowest lows. Thank you for your prayers, emails, phone calls, and visits that let me know I am loved and supported. It truly makes a difference in my life.

Mentors (Cherry Robinson, Dr. Anita Underwood, Dr. Anntarie Sims): To the powerhouses who have served as phenomenal examples of successful women in business, I thank you. Each of you have selflessly poured into me in countless, invaluable ways over the years. It is my full intention to acknowledge you with a humble heart and simply say "Thank you". To whom much is given, much is required. I fully intend to use my gifts to pay it forward.

Christine Kloser: Thank you for coaching me through this amazing process. Your authenticity and genuine love for what you do is inspiring and I am truly grateful for the opportunity to have worked with you!

Shalena "Diva" Broaster: Thank you for all of your support with the birthing of my first book and for being such an amazing business coach! You are brilliant and while I've already learned so very much from you, I know we've only just begun! I believe our meeting in San Diego was divinely orchestrated by God and I am forever grateful. Next stop: Destined For Greatness!

"LM": Without you and the valuable lessons learned from our relationship, much of the content of this book may not have been possible. I always wondered why of all people I had to meet *you*. I know for certain now that our meeting was divinely purposed. Our failed relationship was the vehicle used to drive me into God's presence which would then open so many doors for me. In hindsight I understand exactly why we met, as well why we met at that particular *time* in my life. Everything indeed does happen for a reason. I am grateful to have come out of the experience a much better person than I was going in. Thank you for the life lessons and I wish you the very best! Be blessed always!

TABLE OF CONTENTS

Introduction

Dear Reader,

     Years back I felt called to create a work to help bring both awareness as well as resolution to a prevalent issue plaguing the body of Christ –the issue of heartbreak. There are entirely too many Christians on the sidelines of life -- rendered virtually ineffective in ministry because they are currently trapped in a cycle of hurt. So often, matters of the heart are looked upon as something both inevitable and generally insignificant. The expectation is that because most of us will experience heartbreak at some point in our lives, we may as well learn to deal with its ramifications. Heartbreak can be an extremely significant event. In fact, it is often a quite pivotal moment in a person's life. Some people have the ability to come back from their experience stronger, wiser, and better than ever. Others are not as successful in rebounding and their lives begin a destructible path as a result of their painful situation. The direction in which our lives take after experiencing heartbreak depends greatly upon our willingness to recognize there is a process that *must* take place before we can engage in a new relationship.

     It is my prayer that this book will be the beginning of your deliverance and healing from the painful stronghold of heartbreak. It is my full intent to empower you with my personal experiences in conjunction with Bible-based knowledge that will significantly enhance your journey of discovery. This book is interactive and will require you to be honest with yourself as you pick up the pieces and resume life. However, the ultimate goal is that you resume life not as you once knew it, but more powerful and purposeful than ever.

     Life is an incredible gift and is meant to be lived to the fullest. However, your heartbreak has brought your life to a halt. You are unsure of where to go or what to do next. Your broken relationship has left you in a whirlwind; void of any clear direction. A war rages within and there is little to no peace in your heart. Your esteem of self is significantly low and somehow you've managed to convince yourself that you just lost the best thing in your life; you can't do any better. The anger you feel is so real that you literally wake up with it; like a layer of skin that you are unable to peel off. Your bitterness is intangible but like a virus, quickly spreads to every other aspect of your life. You are bitter at home. You are bitter at work. You are bitter everywhere you go because the resentment you feel is unrelenting. The hurt you've experienced is so deep you can't imagine the day when you will smile or laugh again. Fear of an unknown future has rendered you unable to fathom the possibility of "loving" that deeply ever again. (Please notice the word 'loving' was put in quotations. This is because by the time your restoration process is completed you will know for certain the true definition of what it means to love and be loved. It is highly likely that right now your understanding of love is finite, conditional, and superficial.)

You have found yourself in a situation that you've never experienced before. The depth and breadth of the pain you feel is unprecedented. Although you may not be able to genuinely see how you are going to get through this trial, there *is* good news for you!
The good news is that there is a cure for what you are feeling. The even better news is that although the cure will cost you dearly, it is infallible and 100% guaranteed to get you back on track. As Christians we serve a God who laughs at "impossible" and is able to do exceedingly and abundantly above all we can ask or think. So the first thing you need to know for sure is that whatever the situation, **there is no hurt God cannot heal**. Take the time out right now to give yourself credit for taking a significant step in the right direction.

May God bless you amazingly as you read this book! May the words on these pages speak to your heart and begin to open your mind to the possibilities that await you on the other side of this experience. Everything happens in its due time and season. If you are reading this book, it is clearly your season for change and restoration. It is your time to rise from the ashes of heartache and despair to reclaim your life. Open your heart and believe God for his promises. There is so much in store for you on the other side of this journey and as long as you are ready to do the hard work, you will receive it all! There is no quick fix. You will WORK.

Dorothy

CHAPTER 1: THE END

It must be incredibly strange to begin reading a book with "THE END" as the title of the very first chapter. However, that is exactly where your restoration process begins. Right now you must fully accept and own the reality of your situation, which is that the relationship you were once in has ended. As you accept the truth, you give yourself permission to move forward with this life changing process. The most important thing to remember is that life is cyclical. For every ending there is indeed a new, beautiful beginning. Regardless of the pain you are currently feeling, once you truly recognize this as your beginning, you will garner the strength necessary to accept the ending of your relationship.

Stunned, shaken and *shattered* are words that could be used to describe what you felt in that initial moment. The person you believed was your soul mate is now gone and you fight desperately to control your emotions. As confusion sets in you struggle to find answers to all of the questions running through your mind. Regardless of the details of your specific situation, the reality is that the relationship you once had is in fact over. At this time you aren't certain about much, but you know for sure life as you know it will be changed forever. You are absolutely correct.

COME OUT OF THE EXPERIENCE BETTER AND NOT BITTER.

You've heard it before and you know it to be true; breaking up *is* hard to do. Although it is something we may all inevitably face in our lifetime, a breakup can sometimes be a catastrophic event. Depending on the caliber of the relationship, the breakup can be a shock to your system like nothing you've ever experienced. The blow to your heart can feel like something that can in no way be healed, but fortunately that is not the case.

It is safe to say all breakups are not created equally. Each breakup experience is different, as is its potential impact on our lives. However, what you do next will inevitably set precedence for the direction in which your life will go. In this pivotal moment you have the amazing opportunity to begin a process that will deliver you from emotional, physical, and spiritual bondage. On the other hand, you have the freedom of choice to engage in behaviors that will continue to emotionally, and spiritually imprison you. **The choice is yours.**

It would seem the most obvious thing to do at this point would be to keep reading. After all, you *have* picked up the book with the intention of finding out how to properly heal from a broken heart. Even still, this is actually the point where you need to ask yourself a significantly important question:

ARE THERE LIMITS TO WHAT I AM WILLING TO ENDURE DURING THIS HEALING PROCESS?

The answer to this question is incredibly important. If you have already placed limits on just how uncomfortable you are willing to be during your journey to restoration, you are in trouble. In fact, it is highly unlikely this book will be of help to you. On the other hand, if you have reached a point in your life where you are fully aware that you will have to do something different in order to attain something different—then keep reading. Those of you who are courageous enough to approach this journey with an understanding that it will be one of the hardest, yet most rewarding experiences of your life will have no regrets. Fasten your seatbelts because you are in for the ride of your life!

When it comes to heartbreak the "end" can often feel utterly devastating. This ended relationship can feel like a conclusion, and/or the finale of life as you have come to know it. However, perhaps you should consider the possibility that the "end" was truly only the beginning of something epic? The beginning of something so spectacular and majestic, even the most descriptive words couldn't begin to accurately depict what was on the horizon for you! What if the relationship you were in *had* to end? What if the ending of that situation happened in order to set in motion all of the events that would one day usher you into a place of sheer joy, love, and peace within; a state of readiness for the relationship *God* wants for you?

For such a short and simple word, "end" carries a lot of weight. It is very important to recognize that when dealing with heartbreak, multiple meanings of this very same word can be applicable. In some cases the word "end" refers to the official death of something. Words like demise, decline, and ruin are often used to help accentuate that particular meaning. Your relationship has come to an end and the reason why you feel like you are mourning a loss is because in fact some*thing* has died! A significant bond in your life has been severed and you are feeling the absence of this individual and all they contributed to the relationship (good and/or bad). Putting the details of your personal situation aside, your mind is still registering the end of this relationship as a loss. Something that *was* there is now gone and in many ways it can feel like there has been a recent death of a loved one. Whether this is your first heartbreak or you've experienced it before, it is important for you to be able to define and make sense of how you are feeling.

An "end" can also refer to the remainder of something; perhaps a scrap, remnant, or leftover. You feel like you have been left with pieces and remnants of your former life with that individual. A descriptive analogy would involve broken glass. Something that was once whole is now shattered, fragmented, incomplete and officially useless. However, please keep in mind touching broken glass can be dangerous, and cut you deeply. There is absolutely no need for you to risk yourself harm while attempting to put the pieces back together.

Shattered glass is not meant to be put back together, but simply discarded. It is the same for your relationship at this moment in time.

The word "end" can carry the meaning of a goal, purpose, intention, design, or result. Many often use the phrase, "a means to an end". Challenge yourself to identify this particular meaning of the word from a different perspective. Many times we may not even realize it, but God allows certain people into our lives for reasons and seasons. When faced with heartbreak, we must ask ourselves what purpose these people served in our lives and if in fact they were simply a means to an end. What does that mean? Perhaps the ending of your relationship has ushered you into the exact time and place you were meant to be thus aligning you perfectly with God's design, intention, and purpose for your life. It is very possible that although this relationship failed, you are able to take away a plethora of experiences that actually help to make you a better person. This relationship may have taught you valuable lessons that you needed to learn in order to effectively press forward in your life's purpose.

"End" is also often used to describe the location of something. Edge, base, boundary, tip, and point are all words that can help support the meaning of the word in this particular instance. It is here we are able to recognize the "end" can actually be a tipping or pivotal point. At the end of every relationship, we are at a point where we are on the edge of a new dawning. It is here that you find out if you are courageous enough to jump -- even if you don't know what the landing will be. Consider this to be a pivotal point in your life that will require impeccable decision making and dedication to ensure you come out of this experience better and not bitter.

Finally, the word "end" can be used to describe the conclusion, termination, expiration, or completion of something. It is this meaning in its simplest form that you probably most identify. In your mind, your relationship has concluded, expired, or been terminated. Its shelf life is over and there is nothing that you can do to make the situation any different. Something that was once so incredibly sweet has gone sour and it is virtually impossible for you to return it to its original state at this juncture. The reality is that your relationship has indeed expired. Similar to expiration dates on foods, medicine, and/or drinks we tend to purposely avoid ingesting anything past its expiration date. We have no problem discarding of things that are no longer useful and could potentially be harmful due to past expiration dates. Why then are we so unwilling to not accept the expiration dates of our relationships? Get into the good habit of understanding from the very beginning that not all relationships you have were meant for a lifetime.

The ending of a relationship is always the same result: **two people going their separate ways**. However, the detail of every situation differs and it is important to acknowledge that fact. How each relationship came to the point of no return will differ tremendously. Yet, the feelings of sadness and sorrow are quite universal. If you are willing to be candid, some of you may have seen the end of the relationship nearing before it actually happened. In a situation like that, although you weren't shocked, it didn't hurt any less when the relationship ended. Others may have been "blindsided" by the ending of the relationship. The word blindsided was put in quotations because the truth is that none of us are ever *completely* blindsided when it comes to the ending of close, intimate relationships. We tend to see, hear, and experience what we want while neglecting the reality of our situations in an attempt to hold onto something that God himself may be trying to separate us from.

There is no perfect relationship and each one will undoubtedly experience highs and lows. However, if you are honest with yourself, you may be able to recall a pivotal point in the relationship where you knew for certain this individual was not for you. Some of you may have had relationships that began to cause more strife and pain than it brought joy and you *knew* something wasn't right. Some of you proceeded with the relationship for months, maybe years and as a result lost valuable time you can never get back. Some of you may have ended things right away but still feel the sting of time lost in the relationship. Some of you wanted out but didn't have the strength or courage to end the relationship so you waited for your partner to call things off.

Regardless of your individual situation, the fact remains that there were signs leading up to this event and you must own that in order to continue to move forward in the healing process. What is the purpose of heartbreak and being at such a low point in your life if you are not willing to learn all that you possibly can about how to avoid being in this situation again?

You may have even asked yourself questions like, "Why did this have to happen to me?" "What am I going to do without him/her", and "Did I do everything I could to save this relationship?" These questions are all incredibly valid, but challenge yourselves to press past this stage of inquisitiveness. It is here in the place of questioning and self-criticism that you can waste significant time trying to find the answer to questions of which only healing can answer. In due time, you will have all of the answers you need. Instead, make the commitment to refrain from expending any of your valuable energy focusing on the past and focus on your restoration. The next time you are in the car driving, take notice of something. Your windshield is significantly larger than your rearview or side mirrors. Although it is imperative for you to see what is going on around and behind you, it far more important for you to focus on what lies ahead. That analogy aptly describes your restoration journey.

Your restoration process will require faith, commitment, and patience. In addition, you have to be willing to be honest with yourself at all times. This book was not created to assist you in blaming the other person for the pain you currently feel. If you are looking for a book that will somehow make you feel better about your situation by absolving you of accountability, you can stop reading right on this page. Relationships are always made up of two willing parties. In end the end, someone got hurt and someone did the hurting. As the person who was hurt, it is your responsibility to do whatever necessary to avoid having to learn this same lesson again. There are always signs.

With that said, what were the signs that your relationship was nearing its end? Where did things begin to unravel and go wrong?

- Late nights at the office?
- An email unintentionally left open on his/her personal computer?
- Petty arguments; almost like your mate intentionally wanted to avoid intimacy?
- A sudden onset of secretive, clandestine behavior?
- A genuine feeling of disconnect?
- Physical and/or emotional abuse?

This is a relatively short list and perhaps none, a few, or all are applicable to your past relationship. The significance here is to get you to recognize the importance of identifying the signs as related to *your* specific situation. When dealing with matters of the heart, while our senses are often dulled they are still *there*. Acknowledge and own up to each and every one of the signs you received while in the relationship that this was not for you. By doing so, you will begin to train your mind to identify the warning signs in any future relationships that are gearing up to be a waste of your valuable time. The signs are always there for you. The real challenge is whether or not you are willing to take action once those signs become evident.

RECOGNIZE THE IMPORTANCE OF ENGAGING IN YOUR OWN RESTORATION PROCESS.

Depending on the depth and breadth of the relationship many of us can remain in denial for significant lengths of time without fully coming to a solid understanding that the relationship is over. The truth is, until you have finally come out of the denial phase, you unfortunately cannot begin to move forward with the restoration/healing process. You cannot begin to properly heal a wound that your mind has not allowed you to register as being there.

It is okay to admit the pain you feel from this crippling experience may be unprecedented. Your heart is broken and you cannot see past the pain of the moment. The person you love is gone and the relationship you've worked so hard to make a success has failed. The good news is that this condition of the heart will not last forever and God will restore everything that was taken from you. In Isaiah 61:3, God makes us a promise that it is important for you to remember at this particular time. The New International Version (NIV) reads, "…and provide for those who grieve in Zion—to bestow on them a crown of beauty instead of ashes, the oil of joy instead of mourning, and a garment of praise instead of a spirit of despair." God knows exactly what you are feeling and is committed to helping you heal emotionally. It is important that you take notice of the word "helping". God can and will help you along this healing process, however there is work you must do as well. There is no quick fix here; your restoration and healing will need to be a team effort.

God is love and there can be no confusion about that fact. God is all things beautiful and wants the very best for His children. With that said, sometimes He will allow certain people into your life for a reason and/or season to stir up the waters. These people are not meant to stay forever, but will come to teach you valuable lessons about life, love, and forgiveness. God wants to bless you with a beautiful, healthy, reciprocal relationship when the time is right. However, there is work to be done in order to get you ready for that gift.

The Bible tells us that God has a plan to prosper not to hurt us. Sometimes we will go through various situations in life that will push us to the brink of sanity, test our strength, and exercise our faith. These trials come to strengthen us and we can rest assured God would never put more on us than we can bear. You are stronger than you know right now. The beauty of the restoration journey is that once you are on the other side, the "old" you will be long gone!

Yes, all of these words are extremely poetic and as a Christian, you've heard them all before. In fact, deep inside your heart, you know they are all very true. However, this "feel good" message of God's love, forgiveness, and restoration may not be doing a great job of penetrating your heart right now. You are experiencing a spectrum of emotions and can't get past the pain you feel to even slightly imagine what the future will hold for you. Just be certain God understands how you are feeling, knows what you are thinking, and has the solutions you need to be healed and whole again.

Restoring a broken heart is not simple. In most cases what is actually being restored is a broken *life*. The scope of your entire existence and being is at stake here. A broken heart is never just a broken heart. If we are not careful, a broken heart can lead to broken self-esteem, broken health, broken finances, and even a broken spirit. It is up to you to recognize the importance of engaging in your very own restoration process before considering the possibility of another relationship. There are far too many broken people walking the earth who are emotionally bankrupt, lack self-awareness, and as a result constantly need to be in relationships with others. At the end of the day, these hurt and broken people will only hurt other people. It is a cyclical disaster you can avoid if you are willing to do the hard work required.

Those who are courageous enough to go through the highest highs and lowest lows of the restoration process will truly be victorious as they come out on the other side of this experience. The other side of this heartbreak is: **freedom, forgiveness, gratitude, faith, hope, revelation, clarity, and a new, divine relationship with your Lord and Savior Jesus Christ**. If complete restoration is what you seek, there will be hard work involved. However, this process will lead you in an amazing direction that will catapult your life into a space of limitless opportunity.

Are you ready? Let's embark on this journey together!

Prayer:

Lord I come to you broken, confused, and filled with sorrow. The pain I feel is like nothing I've ever experienced before. Lately I've been feeling like I have nowhere else to turn for the level of comfort I need. I've been wronged and my emotions have completely taken over. Lately I find myself consumed with anger and bitterness. Please help me to both acknowledge and accept each lesson from this failed relationship. Help me to remember for every ending there is yet a beautiful beginning. My relationship with you is not as strong as it should be. Poor decision making, faithlessness, and impatience have all contributed to this extremely low point in my life. As I begin the restoration process please endow me with the strength I need to come out on the other side of this experience completely renewed. I humbly submit to you all feelings of confusion, anger, bitterness, denial, and disappointment. I declare and decree I am exactly where you want me to be at this point in my life. You are all knowing and it is impossible for you to fail. Lord, I trust you and know for certain your plans are to prosper and not harm me. Thank you in advance for the miracles and blessings you will release in the days, weeks, and months to come as a result of my obedience—which your Word tells me is far better than sacrifice. I give you both my hand and broken heart as I accept the challenges that lie ahead on my journey to restoration. I know with you all things are indeed possible.

CHAPTER 1: REFLECTIONS

Your restoration process cannot truly begin until you have accepted the fact that your relationship is over. Take some time to answer the following questions that will help you to better assess your current situation.

1. Have you genuinely accepted that your relationship has some to an end? Is there any part of you that is unwilling to let everything go and begin your healing process? Explain.

   _____

   _____

   _____

2. This process will at times be both painful and uncomfortable. How do you typically deal with uncomfortable situations? Explain.

   _____

   _____

   _____

3. What does 'restoration' mean to you? What are you hoping to get out of this transformational journey?

   _____

   _____

   _____

CHAPTER 2: CRY ME A RIVER

Tears will fall and indeed there will be many. It will be difficult to escape the outpouring of emotion experienced in this phase of the restoration process. Many are unaware of this fact, but there are actual benefits to crying. Scientists have proven crying can help lower your stress levels, stabilize your mood, and even prevent colds by flushing germs that get into our eyes. (You are too upset to care about any of that, but there is always a silver lining. Even for tears!) It is likely you will cry more than you ever have in your life. This reaction to the ending of your relationship is natural and should not be suppressed. You may experience a free range of emotions but most of all an indescribable sadness. The happiness you may feel on occasion is fleeting. More often than not you will prefer to be left alone. It is imperative you recognize and validate your feelings because they are completely normal.

This is where the difficult part begins. There is no crime in crying over the loss of a relationship that was once of great significance to you. The crime is crying without fully identifying exactly *why* you are crying. Ask yourself: What am I crying for? Am I crying because I feel as though I've been deceived and taken advantage of by someone who claimed to love me? Am I crying because I genuinely believed this person was going to be the love of my life? Am I crying because I am fearful that I will never experience love again? Am I crying because I am embarrassed and preoccupied with the thought of facing family and friends; having to answer questions about what went wrong? Am I crying because I feel like a failure after doing everything possible to make this relationship successful? Am I crying because the thought of being alone is so frightening? Am I crying because I am angry with myself for not ending the relationship sooner? Am I crying because I completely let myself go in this relationship and no longer feel attractive?

Whether the list is short or extensive, the reasons you are crying are all your own. They are all valid, uniquely associated with your individual situation, and make perfect sense.

TAKE OWNERSHIP OF YOUR EMOTIONAL SPACE YOU AND HOW YOU GOT HERE.

Crying should be much more than an occasional release of pent up emotion. You must continually identify the reasons why you are crying and validate those tears. The reason you are doing this is to ensure there are no wasted tears. Throughout life you will find that certain problems, issues, and circumstances will continuously represent themselves until you have learned what you need to know. Consistently identifying the reasons you are crying will bring the experience full circle and assist you in learning each valuable lesson intended by God. Crying just for the sake of crying is of absolutely no benefit to you. There is meaning behind every tear you shed and you must endeavor to be keenly aware of each of them.

Your relationship is over and this is the period of time in which you go through what will feel like a grieving process. The fact that you are officially alone sets in during this phase. A song on the radio may send you into a whirlwind; walking down the street and smelling the scent of their perfume or cologne may stop you right in your tracks. This is a pivotal time for you because there are various challenges ahead. For a while you will consider going back to the relationship you left or seeking to get back with the individual who left you. There are those of you who are used to being in relationships and can't honestly remember the last time you were single. The feeling of being alone frightens you more than death itself so this space of "singleness" is uncomfortable to say the least. The naked truth is that some of you will feel more comfortable in an unhealthy relationship than being alone. You would rather argue than sit alone in silence because silence can seem so loud.

Some avoid being alone because they unfortunately associate "singleness" with being unworthy or not good enough. Many also avoid being alone because of abandonment issues from their past that create a need to constantly be surrounded by others. Often, the idea of being alone is rejected because *aloneness* will inevitably yield *awareness*. Ignorance is bliss for these types of people and the less they know about themselves, the less work they have to do in order to affect change. Change is extremely difficult and is therefore often avoided by so many. If you are one of these types of people and are unable to enjoy singleness because solitude frightens you, don't beat yourself up about it. Recognize it for the hindrance it is and know for sure the completion of your restoration process will change this about you. With no uncertainty, you will *have* to go through this process alone.

Social media permeates our existence and we live in the generation of Facebook, MySpace, Instagram, and Twitter to name a few. These outlets literally feed into our narcissism as we constantly post details of every movement along with our best "selfies". Social media allows many to create a false reality and intricately design the message they choose to give the world about how much they love themselves. But as you project the "self" you want others to see, the real question still remains: "Who exactly *are* you?" While some of you have absolutely no idea, others are fully aware. These types of people work diligently each day to mask their true selves because who they are at the core is unsightly and frightening. Yet, the irony here is that although you don't like yourself, you find it both appropriate and necessary to be in a relationship with someone in the hopes *they* will like what *you* don't. That particular mindset is incredibly alarming. If you don't enjoy spending quality time with **you**, why should someone else?

Another color of this spectrum incorporates those who constantly seek to be in a relationship because that is how they best identify themselves. These types of people have a need to be linked to others in order to feel important. They have somehow convinced themselves that without others their existence is less meaningful or significant. Hearing people use phrases like, "I'm nothing without him/her", "I can't breathe without him/her", "I don't know how to go on without him/her", and/or "He/she was my everything" are all indicative of a person's unhealthy dependency on their mate. Your restoration process will reveal to you the importance of having codependent relationships that are mutually beneficial and supporting. You are a valuable, significant, and an equally important member of the partnership. At no point should you ever feel that your life and the joy you experience in it is solely dependent upon an outside source. Most importantly, if you are going to rely on an unchanging source, it must be your Heavenly Father. While people will inevitably fail you due to their natural imperfections, God will not. Whether you are an individual who is simply frightened by the idea of being single, or someone whose identity is dependent on others, please know both situations are unfavorable and will inevitably lead to poor decision making.

Tears will continue to fall as you try your hardest to understand why the relationship ended. For some this time of reflection may yield the resurfacing of what should have been obvious truths about the relationship. For others, the reason for the breakup may be far less obvious because you can't pinpoint the exact moment when things started go wrong. Perhaps there was no fighting, abuse, *or* negativity in the relationship other than the fact that you genuinely did not "click". Consider the possibility it was as simple as God saying, "This is not the relationship I have for you." Maybe the relationship had to end because the person you were with was inhibiting you from carrying out your God given purpose while on earth. Maybe that dead-end relationship served as a blockage to your blessings and God needed to remove him/her from your life. What you must accept is that there is a strong possibility you may never know *exactly* why the relationship ended and why God would not allow it to continue. The only thing you can know for sure is that if the relationship was truly ordained by God, not only would things have "worked out", but it would have flourished!

Nonetheless, the restoration process is officially underway and it is important you be aware of the various challenges that will be presented. The first pitfall to be mindful of is the inevitable "rebounding". This situation happens when we seek out another relationship for the sole purpose of filling an empty void. A lot of us struggle with solitude and would rather be in *any* type of relationship than to be single. We can be often made to feel like something is wrong with us if we are not in a relationship at any given time. However, being in just *any* relationship will not necessarily guarantee happiness and bliss.

TO HAVE SOMETHING YOU'VE NEVER HAD, YOU WILL NEED TO BE WILLING TO DO SOMETHING YOU'VE NEVER DONE.

Getting into another relationship to dull the pain of your most recently failed relationship is a surefire recipe for disaster. The reason "rebound" relationships never work is because you have not gone through the restoration process. You are not yet healed and the only thing you can bring to your "new" relationship is "old" baggage. The only certainty here is more hurt, shame, and guilt compiled onto an already painful, complicated situation. Do yourself a favor and reject the temptation to reach out and latch onto the first person that comes along to help you "get over" the last relationship. If a genuine relationship is what you desire, you will have to complete this life changing restoration process.

There can be no doubt that your happiness is most important. For those who ended the relationship, the brave decision you've made illustrates your unwillingness to compromise or settle for less than deserved. For those who did not end the relationship, just know and accept that God helped make the decision for you. It doesn't seem like it at this juncture, but soon the tears will stop flowing and there will be nothing but gratitude in your heart. You will reach the understanding that your heavenly father blessed you amazingly by ridding you of that relationship. Remember that God has an aerial view of your situation; unlike you, his vantage point is neither skewed nor distorted.

God's thought life is eternal and His wishes are to bring relationships into your life that will prosper you. On the other hand, our thought life is linear and we tend to be concerned most with what is going on right now. This often leads to poor decision making based on a need for instant emotional and physical gratification. God is concerned about every aspect of you. He will absolutely deny you what you want *now*, to give you exactly what you *need* later -- when you are fully ready to receive that gift.

What's most important to remember is that whatever they are, your feelings are valid. Do not buy into the lie that crying is for babies and that your emotions are something you should attempt to hold inside. Without question, the ego will play a role in trying to convince you that you are too strong, too independent, and too much of an adult to cry. Too often when faced with heartbreak we are inclined to believe that if we cry, we've allowed the person who wronged us to "win". This is false and you should reject anything that aligns with that train of thought. The idea is to come out on the other side of this restoration process better versus bitter. Suppressing your genuine emotions will surely lead you to a place of deep-rooted anger and frustration, so let the tears flow. They will do their part to help cleanse your soul and renew the heart. Let nature take its course and continue to push your way through this highly emotional, intensely frightening, yet phenomenally rewarding process of renewal and complete restoration.

One of the only things certain in life is change. You should expect to experience many as you go through this process. There will be a gradual separation from everything you have become dependent upon. Feeling as though you are the only person on earth who really understands the level of pain you are currently experiencing will be difficult. However, during the course of your spiritual development you will learn to depend on and seek God.

It is important for you to remember that while other people may not understand what you are going through, God does. It may be difficult for you to comprehend right now but He knew what events would happen in your life to bring you to this place in time. He is fully aware of the pain you feel and is the only source that can offer you the extensive comfort you seek at this point. Rest assured knowing you are not alone and God will give you the strength needed during this difficult time in your life.

It is in this phase of the restoration process that you are exceptionally vulnerable. For those of you who did not end the relationship, your negative thought patterns will cause you to replay everything in your mind. By doing this, you will attempt to figure out what you could have done differently to make the relationship successful. You may even start to blame yourself for the failed relationship and in doing so, come face to face with deep-rooted insecurities. There is no party like the pity party you can throw for yourself when you have had your heart broken. All of a sudden, you will have very little difficulty managing to convince yourself that you weren't attractive, smart, wealthy, or "good" enough to make him /her stay in the relationship. Every insecurity you've ever had (and even some you never knew you had) will come to the surface. It is here you must remember the devil is the father of each and every lie. He is a thief and will undoubtedly come to rob you of the knowledge that you were created in God's likeness and image; that in fact you were "fearfully and wonderfully made". If you were made in God's likeness and image, how then could you ever be inferior or not "good" enough?

You were made in God's likeness, and because of Jesus' sacrifice at Calvary can come boldly to the throne of grace to ask for what it is that you need. The gift of the Holy Spirit has been made accessible to you, which gives you unlimited access to God's almighty power. Of *course* your spiritual enemy would take this opportunity (while you are at your lowest) to both confuse and discourage you. So many of us go throughout life without true understanding of who and how powerful we are in Jesus Christ. It is incredibly saddening but that doesn't have to be your story.

YOU MAY BE DOWN, BUT YOU ARE NOT OUT!

As the internal battle rages on, the tears will flow like a river and the enemy will attempt to convince you that you are lonely. The idea here is to exploit those of you who always seem to need to be in a relationship and are genuinely frightened by the thought of solitude. There is a significant difference between being lonely and being alone. Individuals who are lonely often feel isolated, secluded, and/or abandoned. Again, this is a **feeling** -- an emotion that you have as a result of the ended relationship. *Being* alone is reality, not a feeling. It is simply a state of being by yourself, on your own, or unaccompanied (in the physical realm). The reason it is important to decipher between the two is because if Jesus Christ is in fact your Lord and Savior then you should know with your whole heart you are *never* really alone. How can you be sure? Because the Word of God says so! In Deuteronomy 31:6, the word reads: "Be strong and of good courage; fear not, nor be afraid of them; for the Lord thy God is with you. He will not leave nor forsake you." Feeling lonely and giving into the fear of being without love for the rest of your life can push you in the wrong direction and lead you down a path of destruction. Be certain to truly understand the difference between being alone and feeling lonely. It is not the same thing and your knowledge of that will assist you in counteracting any whispers from the enemy. This is an extremely pivotal point in the restoration process and requires unwavering, unyielding faith. It is here that you simply need to know what you **know**. Repeat as many times as you need to: "I may feel lonely at times, but I am *not* alone for God is with me."

It's a cliché really. How many situations have you seen people remain in or go back to a negative relationship for fear of being lonely for the rest of their lives? They rationalize staying in the situation because they believe something is better than nothing. Well, here is a secret: A loveless, negative, volatile relationship *is* nothing. It will actually leave you feeling more "lonely" than being single and in a season of consecration with God. Genesis 2:18 reads, "And the Lord God said, it is not good that the man should be alone. I will make a helper suitable for him." For those of you who are in a place where you are tempted to believe the lie that you will always be alone, please know that is not true. God knew exactly what He was doing when he created both woman and man. We were all designed to be connected to other people. With that said, God wants us to be connected to the *right* people. If the enemy can keep you distracted by having you entangled in the wrong relationships, then he doesn't have to worry about you discovering, pursuing, and actualizing your divine purpose. He doesn't have to worry about you using your life to glorify God.

At this leveling point in the process your tears will be innumerable. The anger and hurt you feel inside will almost be unbearable. Your friends and family won't have the answers and although they are there to provide love and encouragement, you will soon find that their efforts are not enough. Although you are at your lowest point, a small voice inside will encourage you to begin to resurrect your prayer life. In keeping with the theme of full disclosure throughout the restoration process, you may be someone who has to admit that your prayer life is virtually nonexistent. Until now, the only time you seemed to have time for prayer was when you found yourself involved in a situation of which you could not escape by your own efforts. You may be embarrassed or ashamed to admit it, but praying is just about the last thing you are interested in doing at this difficult time in your life. However, you will quickly recognize the pain you feel is unprecedented and therefore requires an unprecedented comfort -- something extraordinary and supernatural.

GOD WILL REVEAL HIMSELF TO YOU AS A COMFORTER, A PROVIDER, A SECRET-KEEPER, A FRIEND, AND A PROTECTIVE FATHER.

After you begin to incorporate prayer into your daily schedule you will begin to experience a comfort like nothing you've ever felt before in your life. What is so amazing is that this comfort being extended to you is free, unconditional, and authentic. The beautiful thing about prayer is that it can be done anywhere, in any way, and at any time of day. Prayer is your way of communicating your thoughts, failures, and triumphs with your Creator. Your prayers are not about you letting God in on deep, dark secrets. God is all-knowing and therefore it is impossible to tell Him something He does not already know about you. Your prayers are about admitting you do not have all the answers, but acknowledging a divine source higher than you who does. Your prayers are a declaration to God that you need Him and require guidance to get through any situation.

Be comforted knowing that God hears all of your prayers whether simple or extremely complex. In addition, remember that the Word of God encourages us to keep prayer pure and simple. In Matthew 6:7 we read, "And when you pray, do not keep babbling like pagans, for they think they will be heard for their many words." The idea of prayer should not be intimidating to you. God intended prayer to be one of the most natural and comfortable things we as His children can do.

As the tears continue to flow and your mind begins to change about almost everything, you will start to question life philosophies, lifestyles, behaviors, circles of friends and associates. You will ask yourself, "What changes do I need to make in order to move forward in a more positive direction in my life?" What you should know is that these realizations are all coming directly from God. If they were of you, they would have come long ago. These "epiphanies" you have will undoubtedly be the Holy Spirit ministering to you. Dusting off your Bible and studying the Word of God will help you to understand who He is and what he expects of you. You will find yourself taking complete refuge in the arms of God because that is where you feel safest. During this critical time it is important to remember that although the tears will flow, God will comfort you and soften your heart. Your cries have reached the heavens and you have your Heavenly Father's undivided attention. You cried out and asked God for comfort, peace, and understanding. However, because He is so powerful, He decided to do much more than that for you. The restoration process is officially underway and you will never be the same again. Your tears are not in vain and may all the glory be to God. Change *is* coming!

Prayer:

Lord, I've found myself in what feels like an impossible situation. I am currently saddled with anger and resentment. I've shed countless tears and sometimes I wonder if I will ever stop crying. Help me to understand this restoration process won't be easy. Anything that is restored must first go through the process of being stripped down. Please give me the strength I need to face my fears, and above all else remember there is purpose for this pain. Pain typically signifies something is wrong and requires fixing. My heart is broken but I have faith it will be healed once again by you. Help me to remain steadfast and not allow the perception of lost time to hold me back. In Joel 2:25, Your word tells me that you will restore all of the years the locust has eaten. Lord, I cling to your Word because I know that you are a God who can do everything but fail. That scripture enables me to face anything that comes my way because although I've wasted valuable time in a dead-end relationship, you have promised to give back all that was stolen. Love, joy, peace of mind, and happiness—it is all on its way back to me if I remain obedient to your will for my life. All things happen in due season and right now it is my season of restoration. While this process may be painful, there is no way of expediting what has to happen in order to be restored to my original state of greatness. I trust you completely as I know for certain I can do all things through Christ who strengthens me. Amen.

CHAPTER 2: REFLECTIONS

Tears are natural and cleansing to the soul. Take some time to answer the questions below and reflect on the variety of information you just read throughout Chapter 2. A major part of this healing process will come from your ability to consistently self-assess.

1. In general, do you find yourself holding back tears because you view crying as a weakness? Explain.

    _____

    _____

    _____

2. Do you believe there is value in requiring yourself to 'name your tears' and identify exactly why you are crying? Why or why not?

    _____

    _____

    _____

3. After reading Chapter 2, what is your understanding of the differences between being lonely and being alone?

    _____

    _____

    _____

CHAPTER 3: LETTING GO

Getting over a failed relationship has no set timetable. For some, letting go may take months; for others, it may take years. And believe it or not, some people are unable to emotionally and/or physically let go at all. Some will go throughout their natural life carrying the baggage and emotional scarring of past relationships because the restoration process was avoided. All you need to know for sure is that once you make up your mind to let go, (while not easy) it is *possible*. You will not have all of the answers at once and that is perfectly normal. All you really need is for your heart, mind, and spirit to be on one accord—simply saying "Yes, Lord have your way." Letting go is extremely painful and if we are not diligent, it is here in the process that many of us get stuck for a lengthy period of time. Letting go of the relationship and all things connected to it is typically the stage where fear sets in. You begin to ask yourself questions like:

- Will I ever see this person again?

- What will my life be like without him/her?

- Should I give the relationship another try?

- Why should I let go and let someone else have what I feel is mine?

- Will I have another chance at love?

The idea of never seeing or hearing from this person again may either make you very happy (depending on the situation) or frighten you tremendously. For those of you who have the courage to be brutally honest with yourselves, it may actually do both. After all, you *were* in a relationship with this person. It is difficult to pick up the pieces and move forward without knowing what the future holds. It would be very easy to let go of something if there was certainty you would obtain something significantly better. However, it is here where faith is most necessary. Faith requires being obedient to God's will even when you don't agree, understand, or have the ability to yet see the end result or benefit in what He is asking of you. Throughout the Bible we have numerous examples to illustrate how God feels about faith. Faith is the *only* thing that moves God —not your looks, personality, financial status, educational level, or career achievements. Nothing about you or anything you accomplish in this life will ever cause God to take closer notice of you than your faith.

In the book of Joshua we are introduced to a prostitute named Rahab whose faith was enough to save not only her life, but also the lives of her entire family. Joshua's assignment was to forge his way into the Promised Land and spare no one. However, God was so impressed with Rahab and the faith she exhibited that He spared her *and* her family. Yes, you've read that correctly. Out of all of the people whose lives God could have spared, He chose the town prostitute. How could a not yet reformed prostitute find such favor with the Lord? God took notice of Rahab and rewarded her for her willingness to simply trust and believe in Him.

Faith is mandatory and without it you will be unable to let go of this relationship and *stay* disconnected. The simple act of letting go and cutting ties will disconnect the relationship. However, it is your faith and belief that God has more on the horizon for you that will keep you from seeking reconnection with that individual. You don't know how, you don't know when, and you don't even know whom—by faith you just know God has better for you.

DO NOT WAIT FOR THE "STRENGTH" OR "URGE" TO LET GO.

Similar to skydiving, letting go can be extremely frightening. Before you jump, your mind is racing with thoughts; naturally most of them filled with fear. For those who ask the legitimate question of "how do I find the strength to let go" the answer is quite simple. The answer in its simplest form is a leap of faith. Just take the plunge! Do not allow yourself to be paralyzed by fear. Action is required immediately. There is no *waiting* to be done during your restoration process, only *doing*.

Truly letting go stretches beyond the physical implication of the phrase. It is quite possible to physically be nowhere near the person you've recently broken up with, but still very much holding on to them. Letting go—(and I mean *really* letting go) is an indication to God that you are both obedient and faithful. You have answered His call to either end the relationship or accept that your significant other ended the relationship. In addition, you have acknowledged that while you don't know what the future holds, you trust Him enough to release what you have so that He can replace it with something better. Give a wholehearted "yes" to God's will and prove yourself to be of great courage. Obedience in itself is an act of worship. By being obedient you are telling Jesus that He can be Lord in every area of your life; not just the areas of which you wish to remain in control. If you are willing to be honest with yourself and dissect this recently ended relationship, you will find truth. Any relationship blessed by God will absolutely mirror His definition of love. According to the Word of God, love is patient, kind, not boastful or self-serving amongst other things. If there were elements of your relationship that did not align favorably with God's definition of love, then you can be certain this counterfeit "relationship" did not come from Him. Simply put, God *is* love and real love does not hurt. Ask yourself this difficult question: "Was I in "love", "lust", or "like" just hoping it would one day get to love? Your honest answer to that question will help tremendously as you continue to navigate through your journey of restoration and self-discovery.

Many of us hold onto things we should release and actually release things we should have held onto. There is such confusion when we are not being Spirit led because we are too busy trying to make things happen on our own. However, In 1 Corinthians 14:33 the apostle Paul tells us, "God is not a god of disorder, but of peace". The enemy will undoubtedly attempt to confuse you and make you feel like letting go of this relationship and refusal of reconciliation with that person was a mistake. The goal here is to not only assist you in wasting time, but also distract you from seeking God and aligning with your life's purpose. If you do not disconnect and *remain* disconnected, expect a vicious cycle of break-up, make-up, break up again, and so forth. The only thing you can be certain of in this scenario is the wasting of valuable time. (We will talk about the importance of being an excellent steward of your time in Chapter 12.)

Be vigilant as there will be various emotional snares set for you. The most popular will come on the wings of fear and cause you to resist completely letting go of the relationship. Your hiding place will be under the "just friends" title. Below are 3 different scenarios you should be made aware of:

> **Scenario A:** *The breakup was amicable. You both decided to end the relationship with no hard feelings and you genuinely care for the person. You don't really see why remaining "friends" would be an issue. Well, the answer to that is quite simple (especially if you've been intimate with the person). Friends don't cross certain boundaries. If you were in an intimate relationship with someone, then you've crossed a boundary that you have not crossed with your other "friends". The split may have been amicable, but the only thing you can look forward to if you choose to fall down the "friendship" rabbit hole is mass confusion. While you are being duped by the "we're just friends" ploy, you are inadvertently sending all of your progress thus far during the restoration process into retrograde. Most important to note, while you are busy being "friends" with your ex and falling prey to the occasional idea of taking things to the "next level" again, you are missing chance opportunities to meet the man or woman who was created to love you. There will always be a part of you that is tempted to engage in the extensive list of "what ifs". Please be advised to refrain from using your time to revisit situations from the past you cannot change. Being "friends" with an ex is risky business while you are going through your restoration process. There is always the possibility he/she may find a new relationship before you meet your soul mate. What will happen then and how will that make you feel? How would a scenario like that affect your healing process? There is no way possible for you to be 100% certain of your reaction. Therefore, you need to close the door on the possibility of being set back with insecurities, confusion, and/or bouts of anger. Once you have completed your restoration process you will be of sound mind to assess whether or not you would like to continue a friendship with your ex. Right now, you are emotionally vulnerable and*

therefore susceptible to a host of distractions. Steer clear of the "friendship" trap.

Scenario B: *The breakup was far from amicable but you are afraid to fully let go. You originally started this relationship based on the "potential" you saw in him/her. You waited it out because you were certain one day that individual would become the amazing person you always knew they'd be. You don't want to let go right now because you want to be on the receiving end of this person's greatness. You don't want to close the door completely because if and when they get themselves together you want to reap the benefits. If only this person could learn how to appreciate you and change his/her life around for the better, you would honestly welcome them back into your life wholeheartedly. There are some unfortunate truths that must be addressed for this specific scenario. The first thing you need to keep in the forefront of your mind is that this relationship did **not** end amicably and as a result there is no "friendship" to maintain. According to the Miriam Webster's dictionary, the word potential is defined as "capable of development into actuality." Said differently, one having potential is about the capability of being or becoming something different from what they are right now. There is absolutely nothing definitive about potential. You cannot be sure when or if it will ever be actualized. In this specific scenario, the "friendship until he/she gets it together" trap is self-inflicted physical, emotional, and spiritual imprisonment. You will hold yourself back from receiving God's blessings for you in an attempt to "wait it out" and see what changes time can bring. The only one who will regret this decision is you. True friendship is not contingent upon what we become. Ask yourself, "would I genuinely want to be friends with this person if they never changed a thing?" More than likely, the answer is "no" otherwise you'd still be in a relationship with the person. So if ever faced with this type of situation, identify first and foremost that this person is **not** a friend. Have the courage to let go, and steer clear of this equally vicious and destructive "friendship" snare.*

Scenario C: *Whether the breakup was amicable or not, you can't permanently rid yourself of this individual because you have children together. Those of you who fall into this category will need to be exceptionally careful about how you handle the set "friendship" trap. Nothing can remind you of what **was** more than staring at the beautiful* *face of a child created while in a relationship with that person. You are already contending with emotions on a daily basis as you struggle to co-parent and find mutual ground. Make sure your desire to remain friends is pure with no intention of manipulation or rekindling of a relationship. Here is where you will need to truly understand the difference between successful co-parenting and maintaining a close friendship. It is more than possible to co-parent and engage in cordial communication with your ex for the sake of the children. However, "friendship" when you have not yet gone through your restoration process is a recipe for disaster. Reason being, until you have been fully restored, you are in no condition to receive the friendship of or be a true friend to the person with whom you used to be in a relationship. Right now you are too full of resentment to* **genuinely** *want to be friends with the very person who hurt you. While going through this process, make sure you are always being honest with yourself. Yes, you have children with this individual but you must break all emotional ties for right now. As you go throughout your restoration process, God will let you know if this is a relationship you should breathe life back into by way of genuine friendship. Do not take it upon yourself to make that decision because more times than not, it is a trap that will keep you from your   destiny. God will not send you the man or woman you were meant to be with if you are in any way still holding on to people who are not for you. In order to receive the blessing of the relationship God has for you, both hands must be free to grab onto it!*

YOU MUST HAVE THE COURAGE TO COMPLETELY LET GO AND MOURN THE RELATIONSHIP.

Whether you realize it or not, the "we'll just be friends" phase sends messages to all involved. It tells God—"I don't trust you. I am only willing to let go when I see the physical manifestation of what you have for me. Until I see it, my philosophy is one bird in the hand beats two in the bush. Just in case you don't come through Lord, I have a backup." It tells your former significant other that you aren't *strong* enough to make the decisions that best serve you; that you would rather have some semblance of a relationship than a real love. Finally, (while you may not realize it) the "we'll just be friends" phase actually sends an incredibly strong message to 'self'. You are telling yourself that a piece of something is better than nothing at all. You are silently agreeing with the lie that you are not good enough to have everything you want in a relationship so "friendship" is perfectly acceptable for now. Be very mindful about the messages you send to God, your former mate, and yourself. Your complete restoration and renewal depends upon it greatly.

Anything that starts wrong will end wrong. You may be asking yourself: "How exactly do you *start* wrong?" Anything that starts without God's guidance will end wrong. God wants to be involved in every aspect of your life. Your love life is as important to Him as your health and finances. When you pray, ask that Jesus be Lord of every area of your life, not just the ones you believe you have under control. This will require a combination of both faith and action.

After you make the courageous decision to let go of the relationship, be prepared for some difficult days ahead. On those tough days, a battle will be forged in your mind. Negative thought patterns will work together to convince you that you are somehow missing out on the love of your life. You may also start to believe that you've just let the best thing that happened to you slip away, and no one else will ever truly match the intensity of that relationship. During these times, remember this simple fact: while we make mistakes, God does not. If this person were *for* you, then they would be *with* you. If the relationship ended, it may simply mean that this person was not for you; or at least not right now.

You will grapple with wanting to call and/or email this person for birthdays, anniversaries, or special dates meaningful to you both. You will want to find out what is going on in their lives, or (tell the truth and shame the devil) you may simply want to confirm they are just as sad or miserable about the breakup as you are. Consistent or intermittent contact with this individual in *any* way will undoubtedly facilitate an emotional bond.

The emotional attachment that comes from your inability to completely let go of the relationship can be detrimental. The individual may not be connected to you physically, but without warning you will find yourself in an emotional abyss because of your heart connection. It is important for you to know that your feelings will not go away the minute you make up your mind to let go. Your mind will be filled with thoughts of this person and that is perfectly normal. However, during your restoration process you must remain completely unavailable physically and emotionally to the individual from which you have separated so that you can be *available* to God. God does not wish to share or compete with anyone for your attention.

An unknown author once compared the process of letting go to that of an experience on the jungle gym. As children, many of us remember the experience of playing on the jungle gym, also known as the "monkey bars". While those days of youth have come and gone, we can certainly remember some details of the experience. The main objective was to get from one side to the other without falling or having your feet touch the ground. It was extremely important to hold on as tightly as possible to those bars, even as you feel the weight of your body pulling you down. Depending on your upper body strength, getting across to the other side of the jungle gym was either fairly easy, or took extra strength. Yet regardless of individual prowess and athletic ability to move from bar to bar with great ease or difficulty, there was something every child had to do. In order to move forward, it was essential to let go of the bar you were currently holding.

LETTING GO IS NOT EASY.

Now you may be wondering how letting go of a relationship is even slightly comparable to playing on the jungle gym. Your sentiment is completely understood, mainly because heartbreak and its ramifications are anything but child's play. However, if you look at this analogy a little closer, you will find these two scenarios share a theme of strength, faith, and most of all movement. Your outer strength is what allowed you to hang from the jungle gym and even *consider* moving to the next bar. Your inner strength right now is what has allowed you to get to a point where you genuinely understand the importance of letting go of the relationship. Faith in your abilities sustained you through your fear of falling off of the jungle gym. As a child it was quite possible that your perception of the height of the jungle gym above the ground was incredibly frightening. Fear was a factor because you were afraid to fall to the ground. You didn't know what the results of the "fall" would be -- whether you'd land on two feet or possibly break a bone. In many ways, the uncertainty of the result of your fall was as frightening as the idea of falling. Many of you likely spent extra time holding onto one bar because moving meant the possibility of falling. Similar to the fear you felt back then, today you are faced with the fear of letting go of a relationship to which you have become accustomed. You aren't just afraid of letting go of the individual with whom you've been in a relationship. Part of you is afraid to let go because you do not know what is ahead for you. You can't be 100% certain of your landing. Yet it is here that your faith will both sustain and serve you.

There can be absolutely no forward movement unless you are willing to let go of what you are currently holding onto. As you let go of the first bar and grabbed onto the second, you felt the adrenaline rush. You couldn't believe you had the courage to let go and start moving! As you continued to move across, you started to get the hang of things (pun intended). However, somewhere between the middle and the other side of the jungle gym, you began to flounder. Your legs were kicking, your hands were burning, and your arms were sore from literally pulling and holding your own weight. For a split second there, you'd lost momentum and were afraid again. You looked and saw that it was a long way down. You only had a few more bars to go but you wanted to quit. At some point you even considered just dropping to the ground and taking your chances. Yet, there was a small voice inside that reminded you of just how strong you were and to keep going. You took a deep breath and made up your mind that quitting was not an option for you. You continued to press and although painful, you made it across to the other side. As you stood up on the ladder located on the other side of the jungle gym, you glanced back at where you began and smiled. You couldn't help but feel an overwhelming sense of pride and joy as you reveled in your accomplishment. As a child, this was an incredible lesson for you in tenacity and faith.

As long as you are willing to exercise your faith muscle and refuse to hold onto things God wants removed from your life, you can begin the process of moving forward. It is understandable that you may be afraid and uncertain about what the future will bring. Have faith and be of good courage. God will send you signs and speak to your heart about what is going on in your life. One day you will be able to look back on this time in your life with a genuine understanding of why you had to go through this process. First things first, you must wholeheartedly agree with God that there is much better for you. God has promised us beauty for ashes. Let go of the ashes and look forward to an explosion of miracles in your life.

Prayer:

Lord, please help me to let go. Although we are no longer physically together, I feel myself wanting to hold onto pieces of this individual. Please help me to understand that whatever voids are in my life, only you can truly fill them. Please help me to activate my faith and move forward knowing for certain you are the giver of all good things. Help me to understand what you have for me is better than I could ever imagine. Today I place all of my fears of being single, alone, and possibly never experiencing a true love on the alter. These are all negative thought patterns that are not of You. Please replace these fears with hopes, dreams, and desires for what is to come. If it is your will I thank you in advance for my husband/wife and a relationship that will ignite my soul. As you are readying me, I know that you are also readying him/her. Lord, I trust you and I place this burden of fear down—never to pick it up again. Amen.

CHAPTER 3: REFLECTIONS

Letting go and fully disconnecting from a relationship is extremely difficult. However, this step is not optional when healing and restoration is the desired outcome. Take some time to answer the questions below. Please remember there are no right or wrong answers.

1. What frightens you most about the idea of letting go of the relationship?

   _____

   _____

   _____

   _____

   _____

2. After reading Chapter 3, what is your understanding of why it is essential to avoid being "just friends" with your ex?

   _____

   _____

   _____

   _____

3. How important a role do you believe faith will play in your ability to let go of the relationship? How would you currently describe your level of faith?

_____

_____

_____

_____

CHAPTER 4: THE TRUTH

Many of us may believe the day we accept the fact that the relationship is over, and finally let go means the hardest part is behind us. Try not to get ahead of yourself and know for certain that while letting go was extremely difficult, the next phase of the process can be equally trying. You are not out of the woods just yet. This is only truly the beginning of a lengthy healing process. However, before you arrive at your final destination of renewal, peace, and serenity there will be some unpleasant stops along the way. The best advice to give you at this point is simply to buckle up and get ready. The truth hurts.

YOUR FORWARD MOVEMENT WILL HAPPEN.

With tears streaming down your face you cry out, "Why God? Why did you bring this person into my life if things weren't going to work out?" You are confused, angry, full of questions, and ready to assign blame to God for the pain you feel. However, at this juncture you will need to pause and accept responsibility for the role you played in your own situation. If you are willing to be honest with yourself, you will at some point agree there were signs sent directly from the heavens to alert you this relationship was not for you. Maybe it was that phone number you just happened to find in his/her pocket or that borderline inappropriate email you just happened to glance at when he/she left their laptop open. Maybe it was simply a feeling you had on the inside; a tugging that softly said, "Something isn't right here." On the other hand, maybe you literally had all of the proof any human being could possibly need. You knew for certain the relationship wasn't meant to be and still allowed your fear of being alone to convince you to stay in it.

Before you blame God for "bringing" this person into your life, first understand that you are hurting right now because of the poor decisions *you* have made by accepting this individual into your life, and allowing them to stay once it became clear they should not have that privilege. Women, perhaps you got tired of waiting for the Lord to send you a mate and went looking on your own only to find someone who turned out to be far from "heaven sent". Men, perhaps you got tired of waiting on spiritual guidance to help choose your mate and instead were lured in by her physical features. You had to learn the hard way that a beautiful face and beautiful soul aren't always in direct correlation. You chose not to include God in an extremely important decision and therefore ended up with someone that was not for you. This part of the process is about accepting the truth no matter how uncomfortable or ugly it may be. If you did not consult God or seek counsel from the Holy Spirit before engaging in a relationship, then you automatically left room for error. There is no one to blame for the heartache you feel right now except *you*. The lesson to be learned here is that God needs to be included in your love life.

THE DEVIL IS A LIAR.

The Devil is the author of confusion and the father of every lie ever told. Why is it important for you to know that fact? The reason is because throughout your restoration process, you will be tempted to go back into an area of the wilderness from which God has already delivered you. The "wilderness" is any adverse situation you are facing. It is a trial, a test, or something that feels like a season involving unyielding suffering of some kind. In this particular context, the wilderness would represent your past tumultuous relationship. While that relationship was part of your wilderness experience, this restoration process will be far from easy and will absolutely feel like you are alone in the wilderness again. This time, fighting off lions, tigers, *and* bears.

Don't think for a second you won't be tempted to go back to the very relationship from which God has removed you. The temptation will be consistent as you go throughout this journey. You can be certain the devil is fully aware of the desires of your heart. He knows you seek to be in a relationship and he knows you long to be loved. He will attempt to fill your mind with lies, half-truths, and fear that will cause you to make decisions based on your emotions and negatively influenced thoughts. Below are just a few examples for you to look out for:

- **"It was all my fault"**: What better way to get you to go back to the relationship than by causing you to think the demise of the relationship was because of something you (and you alone) did wrong? If the relationship was meant to be, nothing would have stopped it from being successful, not even the most dire of circumstances.
- **"No one else will want me"**: This is one of the most often used to get you off track. It causes you to question every aspect of yourself and what you have to offer -- your physical appearance, your educational background, your socio-economic status, and your principles. Everything that makes you an individual will be up for scrutiny. There is no better weapon for the enemy to use against you than *you*! Starve this lie with the word of God that reminds you that you are "fearfully and wonderfully made".
- **"I'm too old to start over"**: This lie was craftily designed for the individuals who subscribe to society's norms versus God's will. There are a host of relatively young men and women who feel the pressure to be married with a family by a certain age. Some consider going back to relationships that are no longer serving them because they fear the process of building a new relationship. They realize all good things take *time* but buy into the lie that they don't have the time to start over. There are so many men and women who remain in stagnant relationships God never intended for them because of their insecurity with age and their perception of time. Know that God is the author and finisher of your faith. He knows exactly who He created to love you and how the two of you will meet. Therefore, time is a relative concept. (We'll

discuss that more in Chapter 10) Make up in your mind that while venturing through uncharted waters of a new relationship may take time, your destination will be *new* thus making the journey worth it!

The above examples are geared toward the individual who battles with self-esteem and confidence issues. On the other end of the spectrum it is equally important to warn those who lack humility and have arrogant personalities. Be exceptionally mindful of the ego and its power to keep you from receiving the best God has for you. The example below won't be applicable to everyone, but if it applies to you it is vitally important that you acknowledge the truth about your individual situation.

- **"He/She wasn't good enough for me anyway":** The genesis of this lie is pride, inflexibility, and pretentiousness. Regardless of the mistakes you've made, you will be unable to acknowledge any of them if your ego is steady at work. If only for a second, just consider the possibility that he/she *was* a blessing and perfect match for you. However, right now it is *you* who needs the restoration process. It is *you* that needs to be changed from the inside out so that you will be able to recognize your future mate for the blessing he/she really is to you. Be careful to make sure this type of lie does not permeate your mind or spirit. You were indeed fearfully and wonderfully made, but we are all works in progress. Refrain from spending time exalting yourself above others in a desperate attempt to avoid facing the truth about who you are. The time you spend trying to convince yourself of perfection can be used to ask God for humility and the ability to accept His divine correction in your life.

You will need to be grounded in the Word of God to remind yourself of who you are and exactly how God feels about you. It is impossible to effectively ward off the enemy by simply reading or reciting scriptures from the Bible. You have to allow the Word of God to grow on the inside of you in order to truly embody and live what you are reading. You need to know what it means, how it relates to you, and most importantly how you can utilize that knowledge for self-empowerment. The Bible tells us that we perish most from ignorance; not knowing what we need to know in order to stand firm as believers. We simply do not know how powerful we are as members of the body of Christ and many of us fall victim to the wiles of the enemy for lack of knowledge. Make sure you are actively feeding your spirit with God's word, which is pure truth.

One of the biggest lies you will inevitably encounter is that your partner in this past relationship was the love of your life and you will never experience anything this profound again. This couldn't be any further from the truth. When God takes something away from you, you can expect something significantly better to take its place. God is a god of increase! He is your heavenly father and wants the very *best* for you. He would not take the very best from you and replace it with mediocre. He will spare no expense to give you the desires of your heart. He knows what you want, but He also knows what you *need*.

It may be difficult, but you must get to the point of total surrender and rest in God's truth. The truth is that whatever miracles and blessings have your name on them are on the way. There is no one that can take them from you. God is not man that He shall lie and His word reminds us that if we seek first the Kingdom of God, all other things will be added. He knows you seek to love and be loved. However, His timing cannot and will not be rushed -- not even for you.

This next statement may rub you the wrong way, but truth normally does. God indeed created us all in His likeness, loves us equally, and is accessible to all through prayer. However, He did not endow us all with the same gifts, divine assignments, or *magnitude* of assignment to advance His kingdom. Some of us have such a significant calling on our lives that God will *not allow* us to remain in relationships that threaten the fulfillment of our purpose. Every soul has an intended ministry. God created you in mind with a specific way He wanted you to be of service in the earthly realm, whether it's a ministry in medicine, in counseling, volunteerism, teaching, or music to reach the hearts and minds of lost souls.

Marriage is also a ministry that many people have the privilege to experience in their lifetime. The *truth* is that not everyone on the face of the earth was created to partake in the ministry of marriage. You may not necessarily want to hear the fact that marriage isn't for everyone, especially if you are someone who wants it more than anything else. However, if this particular chapter of the book is about an unveiling of truth, you must be made fully aware that the ministry of marriage was not promised to everyone who wants it and more importantly *when* they want it. Make sure you are in constant communication with God that you may be able to ascertain if the ministry of marriage is something He wants for your life right now, or at all.

After you are certain that a relationship is what God wants for your life, there are important factors to keep in mind. You must seek to be in a relationship of which you are equally yoked with your partner. When you are in a relationship that is unequally yoked, discord and dysfunction are inevitable. The word of God tells us in Corinthians 6:14, "Do not be yoked together with unbelievers. For what does righteousness and wickedness have in common? Or what fellowship can light have with darkness?" It is imperative that you seek a relationship with someone who is like-minded, but first make sure *your* mind is on the Kingdom of God.

Many of you may be asking the question: what does it mean to be unequally yoked? Does that mean we have to like all of the same things, complete each other's sentences, and have no sense of individuality in the relationship? Does that mean he/she has to match my educational level and salary? That is absolutely not the case. To be equally yoked is to have a shared understanding of values and goals. A yoke is simply a wooden bar or frame that is attached to the heads or necks of two work animals (such as oxen) so that they can pull or plow a heavy load. To maintain effectiveness and productivity, back in the day people would simply plow their fields using an equal yoke. An equal yoke was as simple as two mules, two cows, or two oxen together. The purpose of putting the two animals of the same kind together was that they were simply more effective at pulling a straight line. Mixing the animals could possibly get the job done, but would likely yield curved or twisted lines. If we apply this to ourselves, it is understandable why the Bible would encourage us to ensure we are in relationships that involve people with whom we are equally yoked.

Any relationship that involves two people who are not like-minded and are not governed by the same set of values and principles is problematic. Being in an unequally yoked relationship is not what God intended for you. Remaining in a relationship with someone whom you are not equally yoked is in essence holding each other back. God wants something greater for each of you and in order to press forward, you must be separated from anything that could have you mentally, physically, or emotionally bound. God wants to separate you from anything that is hindering you from being your very best self.

Please note there is potential harm in revisiting any relationships with people God has removed from your life and not given you permission to pursue again. The biggest danger in reconnecting with someone you shouldn't be with is the potential to recreate/re-establish ungodly soul ties. We live in a time where we don't often think of the spiritual ramifications of engaging in relationships with people. Have you ever wondered why when you break up with someone (more specifically someone with whom you've been physically intimate) it can be extremely difficult to let go? The reasoning is because the act of sexual relation has spiritually tied you to that individual. In the Old Testament, being married to someone was solidified by the connection of man and woman through the act of sex. The Bible doesn't speak of elaborate ceremonies with bridesmaids, gowns, and reception halls. To partake in the physical act of sex with someone, betrothed you to that individual. It is the exact same way spiritually ladies and gentlemen. You are spiritually "married" or "tied" to the people with whom you engage in sexual relationships.

As mentioned before, the enemy is a deceiver and is great at sending counterfeit representation. Your mate looked, sounded, and felt like everything you'd ever wanted. It seemed to be a real, genuine love because that is what you *wanted* it to be. When you combine the subtle tricks of the enemy, an anxious individual that is overly focused on being in a relationship and a virtually non-existent prayer life (resulting in ineffective communication with God), deception is inevitable. When your prayer life suffers, so does your God-given ability to discern the truth from lies. The enemy knows the desires of our hearts and will often use those very things to pull us further away from God.

Sex is not the only way we are deceived by the devil, but it is often the most employed tactic. We've already established the fact that sex before marriage will inevitably create an ungodly soul tie. Sex was something God designed to take place between a husband and wife. Fully recognizing we are in 2014 and while it may not be the most popular thing to say, it is still truth. The reason we have so many broken, confused people roaming the earth is because they have in fact spiritually tied themselves to so many different people, their souls are fractioned and cannot rest. The reason why you feel like something is missing and/or incomplete when you separated from your partner is because they have taken part of you *with* them. Unfortunately these are pieces of yourself you cannot and will not get back. This is why God prefers sexual relations to take place within the covenant of marriage. He created you as a whole, perfect being. Who are you to knowingly and willingly continue to give pieces of that whole person (created in His likeness and image) away to undeserving people?

The Bible has multiple scriptures to illustrate how God feels about fornication, and as Christians we are aware of many of them. For those who are deeply entrenched and genuinely battle yourselves in this area, perhaps you need to go a little further than scripture and start to incorporate your real life experiences. If in fact you were fornicating in your past relationship and you are willing to be honest with yourself, you may be able to admit there was a point where you knew you needed to get out of the relationship, but couldn't. Without question, fornication helps to build a stronghold of dependency. Do any of these sound familiar?

- "I can't live without him/her."
- "I need him/her."
- "This is the only man/woman for me."
- "I will never love anyone again the way I love him/her."
- "There is just this *connection* I feel to him/her."

Your walk with God is personal and your willingness to adhere to His laws of righteousness is as well. This step in the restoration process isn't about condemning those who are engaging in pre-marital sex. It's about equipping you with knowledge of His truth; not what society is currently projecting and leading many to believe is perfectly acceptable. Christians have the responsibility of helping each other live righteously and talking about those difficult, uncomfortable topics that many often avoid. It is important that you truly understand some of the physical, emotional, and spiritual consequences of engaging in relations with people to whom you are not married. We are able see the physical attributes of our potential partners but have no idea what their spirits look like. For some, if you were able to see that whole picture, you'd quickly reconsider becoming involved.

More food for thought is that you will attract to you what you are and not necessarily what you want. Lustful spirits are attracted to other lustful spirits. Angry spirits are attracted to angry spirits. Broken spirits are attracted to other broken spirits. Instead of trying to figure out why you keep attracting the "same kind of man" or the "same kind of woman", please press forward knowing for certain that you are attracting the mirror image of yourself at any given time. This is exactly why the restoration process is so incredibly important. If you are at a stage in your life where you are willing to admit there are changes that need to be made in your life, have the courage to do so. Until you make those changes you will continue to attract people who are struggling in the same areas as you.

The word of God implores us to sanctify our bodies and make them Holy unto the Lord. Sanctification is literally the setting aside of something to be used for a specific purpose. Given what we know about God, we are fully aware that we were all created in His likeness and image to fulfill a purpose that only we can do. Your body is the resting place of the Holy Spirit and we need to know the importance of what that really means. The Holy Spirit is your guide, your helper, your comfort, and the very gift given to you by God himself to help you while here in the earthly realm. How then can we in full consciousness and understanding view our bodies (the temple of the Holy Spirit) as something that can or should be defiled? We need to understand the importance of sanctifying our bodies and offering them as living sacrifices to the Lord. We will never be perfect, but plainly put there are things we should and shouldn't be doing. Learn to ask God for the strength required to resist temptation and maintain righteousness. In James 4:7 the Word tells us to "Submit yourselves then to God. Resist the devil and he will flee from you." Be wise in knowing that the enemy can do nothing without God's permission. God will never allow you to be tempted by something stronger than what you can handle.

Your relationship with Christ is personal and there is nothing more life changing than being in direct contact with Him. Seek God earnestly and you will find truth. Try as you may, there can be no restoration without the acknowledgement and revelation of truth regardless of how unfavorable it may be. Seek the truth, find it, and own it. If it is a "truth" you do not wish to be part of your life any longer, get about the business of changing that particular situation. Your full restoration depends on it.

Prayer:

God I come before you ready and willing to lay all of my truth on the alter. Lord you are my rock and my salvation. I have done many things to make you question my loyalty and willingness to serve. As I repent today of each and every known sin committed, I humbly ask that you reveal those of which I am unaware that are hurting our relationship. I will never be perfect, but in you I have been perfected. I accept this journey and am filled with gratefulness to know your plans for my life are greater than anything I could have imagined. Lord, grant me the courage necessary to face truth as you reveal these things to me. Help me to gracefully accept your correction no matter how much it may hurt. Thank you for the strength you give me each day to resist temptation and that you love me enough to never allow me to be tempted with more than I have the power to resist. It is so difficult living in a world that readily accepts, permits, and promotes the opposite of everything you've created me to be. Help me to live a life that serves as a beacon of light to those who have lost their way. I thank you in advance for the overflow of miracles that will come as a result of this restoration process. Amen.

CHAPTER 4: REFLECTIONS

Truth-no matter how unfavorable, is always the best way to go. Take the time to answer the questions below regarding the truth about your individual situation.

1. Write down 3 "truths" about your current or past relationship. (Regardless of how uncomfortable it may be to do so)

   _____

   _____

   _____

2. After reading Chapter 4, what is your understanding of being unequally yoked? In your own words, why is being equally yoked with your partner important to you?

   _____

   _____

   _____

   _____

3. What are some of the *real* reasons that kept or are keeping you from ending a relationship that is no longer serving you?

   _____

   _____

   _____

   _____

CHAPTER 5: PERFECT VS. PERMISSIVE WILL

While going through the restoration process your mind will be filled with questions and most of them will begin with the word 'why'. There is no specific or set time in which God will reveal "why" he allowed you to experience the ending of your relationship. However, you can be certain as time goes by, you will gain more and more revelation about who you are, who God is, why this experience happened, and how it was intended to prosper you. Yes, prosper you! Most often the word 'prosper' is associated with economic success. However, the actual meaning of the word prosper is "to become strong and flourishing". Therefore, the question is not, "Why did this happen to me?" but, "What life lessons were to be learned from this experience to make me stronger?"

This is the perfect time for you to learn about God's permissive versus perfect will. God's perfect will is what He had planned for you long before you came into physical existence. Jeremiah 29:11 reads, "For I know the plans I have for you", declares the Lord, "plans to prosper you and not to harm you, plans to give you hope and a future." It is important you genuinely understand that you being here at this time, in this place, and of your specific generation was no accident. You were created for a time such as this and there was absolutely a plan for your life before you were born. In God's perfect will, every aspect of your life would be a genuine reflection of your submission to God's sovereignty. Your life and everything about you would be in accordance with God's Law. The result would be the manifestation of undeniable favor in every area of your life. To be within the guidelines of God's perfect will, you would need to be completely obedient to the directive given from the Lord.

The reality is that because we are imperfect beings and each day of our lives engage in the battle between good and evil, many of us are living *outside* of God's perfect will. Our disobedience and unwillingness to submit separates us from the perfect will of God. If you are not in alignment with God's perfect will, then you are within the realm of His permissive will. God's permissive will is simply what He will *allow* you to do with your life. God is love and absolutely wants the very best for you. He will never force your worship, praise, or obedience. However, while God loves us regardless of our many imperfections, living outside of God's perfect will has its consequences. Simply put, there is a divine covering that cannot exist when you are not in alignment with God's *perfect* will.

You may be asking yourself, "What does this have to do with my recently ended relationship?" You can be certain if your relationship has recently ended, then that relationship was absolutely not part of God's perfect will. Your relationship was simply something God *allowed* you to experience. It was a relationship you entered, without God's permission and therefore it automatically lacked His covering. However, the Apostle Paul reminded us about God's grace in Romans 8:28 "And we know that in all things God works for the good of those who love him, who have been called according to his purpose." We serve a God who is ready and willing to extend both grace and mercy to those who love Him. Just because you stepped out of God's perfect will and engaged in a relationship that He did not approve of does not mean you can never realign yourself with His plan for your life. When the Apostle Paul reminds us that 'all things work together for the good of those who love him', he is reminding us that even those situations in life that end up "bad" can be used for "good" by God.

My personal testimony may differ from yours, but this literary work has been written with the intention of remaining as open and truthful as possible. Prior to my most recently ended relationship, attending church regularly, making an effort to ensure my prayer life was consistent, or reading the Word of God to feed my soul were really not on my list of priorities. It is painful to admit, but there were virtually no open lines of communication between me and my Creator unless a dire situation presented itself. In hindsight, I realize relationship with my ex-boyfriend was in no way part of God's perfect will for my life. However God was able to use even *that* situation for good and draw me closer to Him.

Everything in me knew this relationship was not what I needed to be engaging in at the time. By the time my relationship ended, there was such emotional damage it was virtually impossible to find comfort in anyone other than my Lord and Savior. Even at my lowest point emotionally there was a genuine determination to seek the silver lining of the experience. It was at this point in my life that I learned how to lean into and draw strength from my faith. It was amazing to see my faith increase over time. Something that had initially started out so small and fragile grew into something powerful. In my most reflective state, it is clear to me that particular relationship was part of God's permissive will. God did not approve of that relationship, but He used that adverse experience to usher me into His presence. That relationship helped to promote personal growth in ways never thought possible. Prior to that experience, my relationship with God was very inconsistent. My prayer life was mediocre at best and attending church throughout the year was the furthest thing from my mind. In all honesty, church consisted of New Year's Eve service, possibly Easter Sunday, and the unfortunate occasion of a funeral. However, as my relationship with God flourished, there was more consistent prayer, church attendance, and reading of the Word of God. As my knowledge of God increased, so did my knowledge and understanding of myself.

As Christians, the God we serve is omnipotent and there is nothing we can do to surprise Him. With one eye in today and one in tomorrow, the element of surprise is virtually impossible. He is fully aware of the decisions you will make throughout your life and how each of them will affect you. As your heavenly father, He indeed prefers you experience a life free of pain, hurt, and/or agony. However, even as youth raised by our *earthly* parents, there were often consequences that came along with impatience and disobedience. God is really no different. For every action, there are consequences. More importantly, when we are engaging in relationships that we *know* we shouldn't be in, why is there such astonishment when things don't work out? While your past failed relationships were not part of God's perfect plan, they were permitted for a reason. There was a valuable lesson (or two, or twenty) that needed to be learned from the relationship. God knew the trouble within those relationships had all of the makings necessary to help you course correct and seek out His perfect will for your life.

If you are honest with yourself, you may be able to admit that sometimes you need to learn the same lesson multiple times. Every lesson is not constructed equally and some are far more painful than others. Even still, you can go forward in utmost confidence knowing that each trial (regardless of severity) was *allowed* by your Heavenly Father to make you a better, stronger person. Unfortunately, many of us are running away from God instead of running toward Him. We have gotten away from prayer, meditation, and most importantly being obedient to the directive we are given spiritually. We seek His counsel, ask Him to guide us in the right direction, and help us to submit to His will. However, what many of us are really asking is that God submit to *our* will! If that is the case, why do we ask God to reveal his plan for our lives if we have no intention to take any of it into consideration?

GOD'S SOVEREIGN PLAN WILL ALWAYS SUPERSEDE EVERYTHING ELSE.

The amazing thing is that there are some things God has pre-ordained and will come to pass *regardless* of what course you take in life. There are particular events that must happen in your life for no other reason but because God has decreed it so. For those situations, there is absolutely nothing you can do (or not do) to alter the end result. If it was in God's sovereign plan for you to get married at 44 and have your first child at 45, then that's exactly what will happen. When God has a specific assignment, purpose, gifting, or life event with your name on it, nothing can keep you from it. Not even *you*! Some of you may have genuinely bought into the lie that this past relationship was "the one" and can't seem to understand why it was so unsuccessful. The answer in its simplest form is this relationship was not part of God's perfect will for your life. However, since you went ahead with the relationship, He used it to help catapult you to exactly where He wants you to be at this time in your life; seeking restoration, and fully committed to keeping your appointment with destiny.

There are some people who genuinely have difficulty submitting and following instructions. These types of people must go through hardship in order to learn the intended lesson. Sometimes we receive warnings, but fail to adhere to the suggestions made. It is my firm belief that relationship breakdowns do not happen spontaneously. First, second, and third warning signs are given before everything gets completely out of control. Many times you simply disregard the cautionary signs that are presented. In the end, you are saddled with sorrow and regret due to your inaction. What starts out as a bright sunny sky, eventually turns cloudy. Next, you began to smell the rain coming. At some point you may have even heard the sound of thunder off in the distance or saw it flash in the sky. But for some strange reason, none of these signs moved you to take action and seek shelter. After you've ignored each of the indications, the inevitable torrential downpour began and you were soaked from head to toe. This is exactly what happens to us in life when we fail to pay attention and be proactive about our relationships.

I've often had to learn the hard way but in retrospect, there were so many warnings given early on in my last relationship. Sometimes when we feel entitled to something; genuinely believing it is our time for it and we've waited long enough, there can be no stopping us. I knew for certain God did not approve of my relationship at that time. My hope was to somehow change God's mind (as if that were possible). Each and every day my spirit gave a resounding "no" to the relationship. It lacked a foundation of friendship, morality, equality, love, trust, and mutual respect. It lacked GOD. And yet, I ignored all that was going on inside of my mind to satisfy a need and longing in my heart.

One day, my boyfriend at the time, and I had just finished arguing. I cried because I was completely overwhelmed with sadness and confusion regarding the incident. It just seemed like nothing in the relationship ever went right for too long. In that moment I quietly prayed, "Lord if this man is not for me, please just give me a sign." Less than two hours later I received a knock on my front door that would give me the answer of all answers. For some strange reason, that answer (which I know for certain was directly from God) was not enough. I continued this relationship for about 8 more months until finally the walls caved in and I was left surrounded by destruction. I was in such a dejected emotional state that there was literally nowhere to go but up. It is imperative that you genuinely seek to always be in agreement with God's perfect will for your life. You can save yourself valuable time and emotional upheaval by doing so.

The GPS navigation tool can serve as a great example to help further illustrate the difference between God's permissive and perfect will. At the beginning of a road trip, you typically provide the GPS navigation system with all of the information needed to get you to your final destination. The system then prompts you for the street address, city, state, and possibly zip code. Once you provide all of that information, the system will yield directions. The directions will consist of a route that the system will use to guide you to where you need to go. This particular route generated by the navigational system is based on what best fits your needs. The GPS has taken into account the shortest route, least traffic, and tolls to ensure a ride with minimal interruption. If by chance you accidentally or purposely go a different way, the system will provide you with an alternate route to get to the same destination. While the new route will get you to the same destination, you will not be traveling the exact same way it originally planned. As a result of being rerouted and straying from the original plan, you may encounter heavy traffic, inclement weather, unexpected tolls, and/or a longer trip overall. It is the exact same way when we operate in God's permissive versus perfect will. With grace and mercy, you may eventually get to your original destination. However, that doesn't mean you will get there on time or without incident.

We need to begin to consistently ask ourselves how we can be in alignment with God's will. Throughout the New Testament, the prayer life of Jesus Christ served as a great example. Time and again Jesus was quoted as praying, "not my will father, but your will be done." As Christians you are familiar with the many unfavorable situations throughout Jesus' ministry on earth. Even still, we see Jesus submit to the will of God versus His own. That is indeed the same expectation God has of each of His children. God will not interfere with our decision making; He is not a bully. He has given us life along with the gift of free choice to obey or disobey. As Christians it is our responsibility to have consistent communication with Him and seek direction.

DELAY DOES NOT MEAN DENIAL.

The biggest problem is that many of us have been able to convince ourselves that when it comes to matters of the heart, we know more than God. We have these lofty ideas of how we want our lives to go and have taken the liberty of planning everything to the tee. When things aren't moving fast enough, we go about the business of creating and manufacturing the things we desire. However, just because you have yet not received the blessing you've been waiting for, does not mean it will never come. James 1:3-4 reads, "…knowing that the testing of your faith produces patience. But let patience have its perfect work, that you may be perfect and complete, lacking nothing." If God granted every desire of your heart precisely when you asked for it, how then would you ever learn to be patient? We must learn how to both hear and accept the "no" that resounds in our spirits at any given time. "No" does not mean never. The "no" could be God's way of saying:

1. This relationship will end badly and cause you unnecessary pain. NO.
2. This is a relationship you are not ready for just yet because you have maturing to do. NO.
3. You are a man/woman after my heart and I know your desire to be in a loving relationship. However, this person is simply not for you. I have a much better match for you! So for right now…NO.

To be in direct alignment with God's perfect will requires a level of faith and discipline that many of us haven't yet attained. To be candid, it is a level many of us may have no real desire to reach. We have somehow bought into the lie that being in alignment with God's will sentences us to a lifetime of boredom, or longing for excitement. The truth is there can be nothing more exciting than having a solid relationship with your Creator and being in awe as you experience one miracle to the next. Your earthly presence is nothing more than preparation for what you will be doing in eternity. God wants you to have an amazing life. However, God knows we are imperfect beings and struggle each day in the ongoing battle of good versus evil. He knew there should be a Plan "B" (otherwise known as His permissive will) for those who stray from his perfect will.

Only when we fulfill His perfect will can we inherit the complete fullness of the blessings he has reserved for us. Forsaking God's perfect will and operating in His permissive will limits the amount of blessings, peace, and joy in our lives. It requires a strong willingness to align perfectly with what God wants from us. The truth is that it is often just much "easier" to make our own decisions without counsel from God. Exhibiting patience and waiting for blessings that seem to be taking forever to manifest is difficult! However, if you've been blessed to live long enough, you have come to know that anything worth having does not come easily. There are rewards to operating in God's perfect versus permissive will. You must be willing to try it for yourself.

It is equally important for you to understand that some decisions you make will yield irreversible ramifications. There will be no way possible to rewind time and get a "do-over". Some people are far more compulsive than others and quite enjoy living on the edge. These types of people have no problems with "facing the music" and dealing with consequences as they come. Make no mistake about it, there is nothing at all wrong with being a bold, risk taker. However, the purpose of this particular chapter is to get you to fully understand the importance of communicating with God to find out what His will is for your life. There are real life consequences to operating in the permissive versus perfect will of God.

We can use Moses as an example to show God's disdain for blatant disobedience. Prior to the coming of Jesus Christ, no one man did more to advance the kingdom of God than Moses. His faithfulness to God in the Old Testament was without comparison. However, his departure from God's perfect will yield a denial of entering the Promised Land. In Numbers 20:2-13, we read the story of how Moses struck the rock, but failed to give God the credit for the miracle. God's sole purpose for the miracle was to get the Israelites to understand He was the one true source of all of their blessings; not man. Moses disobedience posed a serious problem and as a result, God decided to appoint Joshua to lead the people into the Promised Land.

How does this story in the Bible relate to us? Simply put, our contributions to the Kingdom of God will likely pale in comparison to Moses. If God saw fit to hold Moses to such a high standard of obedience, then certainly he expects equal or better from each of us! Ask yourself the difficult question: Am I making "God" choices or my interpretation of "good" choices based on what I want and when? Your ability to make the necessary changes and get in alignment with God's will for your life depends heavily on your willingness to be obedient. Operating in God's perfect will releases favor and blessings in your life that you've never imagined. Go ahead and give it a try!

Prayer:

Lord, I am wonderfully blessed to have such a patient, loving, and kind Heavenly father. I have had to learn many hard lessons in life due to my disobedience. Thank you for the grace and mercy you've shown even during the raging of storms that were directly caused by my unwillingness to heed to your voice. Today, my prayer is of total surrender. I seek to be in complete alignment with your will for my life. I know for certain that my wildest, best, and most exciting dreams cannot compare to what you have in store for me. Help me to be patient and remember that everything will ultimately happen in its perfect season. Amen.

CHAPTER 5: REFLECTIONS

Take a few moments to reflect on what you've just read about God's permissive versus perfect will. Use the following questions to help facilitate deeper thought on this highly important topic.

1. **After reading Chapter 5, what is your understanding of the difference between God's permissive and perfect will for your life?**

    _____

    _____

    _____

    _____

2. If you are currently operating outside of God's perfect will for your life, what consequences have you experienced as a result? List a few.

_____

_____

_____

_____

3. As a Christian man/woman, how do you actively exercise your faith muscle each day? Explain.

_____

_____

_____

_____

CHAPTER 6: FREEDOM IN FORGIVENESS

Often times when we think of the word "freedom" we associate it with a physical state of being. We've convinced ourselves that if we are "free" then we are able to maneuver due to an absence of physical restraint. However, you must begin to challenge the definition of freedom as you know it. Consider the fact that it is more than possible for your physical form to be "free" while experiencing profound levels of mental and emotional slavery. After you've ended a relationship (especially if it did not end amicably) there is a period in which you are completely submerged in a sea of unforgiveness.

To forgive someone is simply to cease feeling resentment. When you make the courageous decision to forgive, you are neither in agreement nor acceptance of the wrong that was done to you. You are making a statement to yourself, the person to whom you are extending forgiveness, and the universe that you will not spend another moment of your life being held emotionally hostage. You are illustrating your understanding that you do not have the ability to modify the past and therefore refuse to allow the situation to adversely affect your present or future. So many people allow their egos to convince them that forgiving people who have done something to hurt them connotes weakness. The truth is that it takes exceptional strength and courage to forgive others, especially when they show no remorse for what has been done to you.

As Christians, it is God's law that you remain in a constant state of mercy and forgiveness. Each time we recite the Lord's Prayer, we are asking that God "forgive us our trespasses as we forgive those who trespass against us." Many of us are doing an excellent job of reciting this prayer on a regular basis. However, we are failing to genuinely comprehend what the prayer really means! We are asking God to forgive us for the countless sins we've committed and the ways we have offended Him by our disobedience. Micah 7: 18-19 reads: "Who is a God like you, who pardons sin and forgives the transgression of the remnant of his inheritance? You do not stay angry forever but delight to show mercy. You will again have compassion on us; you will tread our sins underfoot and hurl all our iniquities into the depths of the sea." That scripture serves as a powerful reminder of how God faithfully forgives our sins and shows compassion, of which we are undeserving. Truth be told, we should all be grateful to serve a God who is a confidante, corrects us in private, and doesn't keep tally of our many faults.

If people only knew some of our deepest secrets we wouldn't be so quick to judge others. We go boldly before the thrown of grace and on bended knee confess our sins with the expectation that by the time we get up, the blood of Jesus Christ will have prevailed and our sins forgiven. In our minds, the faith we have as Christians makes it just that easy. And yet when someone offends or hurts us, the concept of forgiveness is suddenly far more complicated. We yield to our negative emotions and create fertile ground for the sowing of anger and bitterness. The real question we must ask ourselves as Christians is why we expect to be forgiven without having to exhibit the very same mercy and grace provided to us by God.

In Matthew 18:21-35, Jesus shares with Peter a parable about an unmerciful servant. Jesus often used parables to teach and this instance was no different. Peter had come to Jesus and asked, "Lord, how many times shall I forgive my brother or sister who sins against me? Up to seven times?" Jesus answered, "I tell you, not seven times, but seventy-seven times." Jesus wanted Peter to know he should be willing to forgive on *countless* occasions if necessary. Jesus then went on to drive the point home by using a parable to illustrate the importance of forgiveness and consequences of being unmerciful to others when you have been extended grace on multiple occasions. In the parable, we see a master take pity on a servant and forgive him his debts. The servant did not reciprocate the mercy he was shown by his master to the person who owed *him* money. The news of the hypocritical servant's actions got back to the master. As a result of the servant's unwillingness to pardon someone else after being shown mercy himself, the master turned him over to the jailers and permitted torture. God wants you to forgive others as He consistently forgives you. With that said, technically you do in fact have the free will to choose not to forgive those who have wronged you. However, it is imperative you thoroughly understand how your unwillingness to forgive has consequences.

COMPLETE FORGIVENESS IS GOD'S LAW AND EXPECTATION.

Unforgiveness aids in the maintenance of a relationship with the person who hurt you. You may be saying to yourself, "How is this possible? Our relationship has ended and I am no longer with him/her." Physically you are no longer with the individual. However, where there is unforgiveness, there is also emotional linkage and mental imprisonment. Essentially, you are spiritually paralyzed by the strongholds of anger and bitterness. This then helps to facilitate your inability to move forward with your life. The emotional ties that stem from unforgiveness can and should be compared to that of a jail or holding cell. In reality, the relationship has ended and you now identify this individual as part of your past. However due to unforgiveness, you lack the ability to enjoy the present or look forward to what the future holds because your mind has been detained. The good news is that the length of this prison sentence is entirely up to you. Your freedom will come the minute you make the decision to forgive.

When you forgive those who hurt you, you free yourself from the bondage of anger and resentment. However, you also free the person who hurt you into the hands of God. As long as you hold onto the grudge, and rack your brain with thoughts of revenge you get in God's way. Once you forgive, you are in essence giving the person and situation to God to handle completely. The act of forgiveness is never optional where God is concerned. It is a requirement and expectation of you. Forgiveness facilitates the strengthening of your relationships.

In Romans 8:38-39, The Apostle Paul tell us: "For I am convinced that neither death nor life, neither angels nor demons,[a] neither the present nor the future, nor any powers, [39] neither height nor depth, nor anything else in all creation, will be able to separate us from the love of God that is in Christ Jesus our Lord." What he is in essence trying to tell us is that God loves us in a way that is unfathomable. His love is all-encompassing and everlasting. Nothing can separate us from Him! Christians know this to be factual but that should not stop us from seeking to understand the truth. While nothing can separate us from God's love, unforgiveness can and will separate you from an abundance of blessings. To be unforgiving to others while expecting forgiveness from God is hypocritical.

Forgiving others for their transgressions will keep the lines of communication between you and God open. When you are willing to let go of things God never intended for you to keep, you are saying to him: "I trust you." And, the more you trust Him, the more He can trust *you*! There is a maturity that comes along with learning to forgive people who have hurt you. The more you mature and are able to show God your willingness to grow through painful situations, the more He can trust your decision making. In addition, by forgiving immediately you are ensuring the enemy has no power to enter the situation and hold you emotionally hostage. In Ephesians 4:26-27, the word reminds us: "In your anger do not sin": Do not let the sun go down while you are still angry, and do not give the devil a foothold." We have to be careful not to hold on to grudges because it gives the devil the perfect opportunity to exploit those emotions. You could be having the most beautiful day ever and all of a sudden something happens to remind you of someone who hurt you. Before you know it, your joy has been compromised. There is an almost immediate shift in your mood and disposition. When you forgive, you take the stinger out of the bee; you render that person or situation harmless to you. Something may in fact happen to trigger a memory of that individual, but when you have truly forgiven, that person will no longer be a source of pain.

FORGIVENESS ISN'T ONLY FOR THOSE WHO HAVE HURT YOU.

Some of us actually need to forgive ourselves! Many of us have repeatedly operated outside of God's perfect will for our lives and as a result have subjected ourselves to many painful situations over time. When you are truly engaged in the restoration process, honesty is not optional. You should continually ask yourself what role you played in these unfavorable experiences. You must then accept responsibility, and forgive yourself. The practicing of self-forgiveness goes much farther than your most recently ended relationship. When you forgive yourself for any decision that caused you harm, you are in essence saying to yourself: "You let me down, but I forgive you. You made a poor judgment call, but I forgive you. You failed me, but I forgive you." The relationship you have with God and yourself are really the only ones that will inevitably last for the remainder of your life. We must be willing to invest everything to ensure the relationships we have with ourselves are healthy and fulfilling.

Each day, tell yourself unequivocally: "I love you. I forgive you. I trust you." People who don't love, forgive, or trust themselves often find themselves in extremely dire situations.

"I LOVE YOU"

When we don't love ourselves, we tend to seek love from anyone, anywhere, and for any length of time that it is available to us. This is how you can spend 2 or 3 years involved in a relationship that you *knew* wasn't going anywhere. If we don't love ourselves enough to know for sure that we deserve the best life has to offer, we fall prey to these types of relationships. Therefore, if you don't truly know yourself, how then can you love yourself?

Get into a daily routine that involves mandatory time alone with yourself. Fall in love with every aspect of you -- flaws and all. Each day, make certain to do something for yourself that aligns favorably with the statement of "I love you". As you wash you face or brush your teeth each morning, pause in the mirror and speak to your reflection saying, "I love you." Let go of the negative self-talk and begin to incorporate daily activities that edify your soul and boost your esteem of self. If you don't truly love yourself, why are you genuinely expecting for someone else to be able to do so?

"I FORGIVE YOU"

Some of us find asking for forgiveness from God very difficult depending on the nature of the offense. Christians know and believe Jesus' sacrifice at Calvary for sins of the past, present, and future. While it may be difficult at first to ask God of forgiveness, we often find the strength to do so. In addition, many of us find it just as feasible to ask those whom we've wronged for forgiveness. It may take a while if emotions get in the way but eventually we are able to communicate our wrongdoing and ask for forgiveness. We also find it quite possible to forgive people that have somehow hurt us. However, for some unknown reason, we often refrain from providing ourselves with those same levels of grace and mercy. It is often extremely difficult for us to truly forgive ourselves.

When there are situations in our lives for which we have not yet forgiven ourselves, there is almost always a manifestation of self-destructive behavior. We subconsciously do things to hurt ourselves because we have not forgiven ourselves for past mistakes. When you look in the mirror each day and say "I forgive you", you are not giving yourself permission to fail repeatedly. Often times we can associate forgiving ourselves with condoning poor behavior or lack of accountability. This is not the case at all. You are simply acknowledging that you are human and will undoubtedly make mistakes from time to time. You are also making a declaration of independence from any guilt or shame associated with the offense.

THERE IS POWER AND FREEDOM IN FORGIVENESS.

The significant amount of energy needed to hold onto resentment toward yourself can be exhausting. Every ounce of energy you give to dwelling on past mistakes will ultimately steal from the energy you need to become a better person. Be careful not to waste any time holding yourself back. If God has forgiven, why is it so difficult for you to forgive yourself? Life is full of choices and from time to time we will inevitably make the wrong decisions. Ironically, it is not always the wrong decision that sets us back. Often, it is our inability to forgive ourselves, and move on having learned a valuable lesson from the experience. Forgiving yourself is not a sign of weakness. In fact, forgiveness is a choice that takes significant strength. Above all else, forgiving yourself provides the opportunity to begin the healing process and overcome that difficult situation versus remaining a victim of your very own scorn.

When we refuse to forgive ourselves for our past mistakes it can also be viewed as an ugly form of pride. The Merriam-Webster dictionary defines pride as "a high or inordinate opinion of one's own dignity, importance, merit, or superiority, whether as cherished in the mind or as displayed in bearing, conduct, etc." When we can find it within ourselves to forgive others, but lack the ability to extend the same courtesy to ourselves, we are being prideful. In your mind you are affirming your mistake is somehow much worse than everyone else's. Why have you created a different set of rules; a different standard of behavior for yourself? What makes his/her cheating, lying, or stealing more forgivable than yours? Has your ego convinced you that succumbing to temptation and exhibiting poor decision making skills is somehow beneath you? Have you managed to convince yourself that because you are so much better than everyone else, you *should* be less capable of making mistakes than others? Does your pride tell you that you are smarter, more careful or perceptive than others? Are you harder on yourself because you believe you are so great that you should never fall prey to the same human behaviors as others? These are extremely important questions to answer. When we reject the forgiveness extended to us by God and continuously refuse to forgive ourselves, the result is victimization of our own pride. Proverbs 16:18 reads, "Pride goes before destruction, and a haughty spirit before a fall." Pride has no rightful place in your restoration process. It is the antithesis of every good personal quality you are working diligently to enhance. Author and political activist Ralph Nader once said, "Your best teacher is your last mistake."   Every mistake you make is yet another opportunity to learn a valuable lesson and help to reshape your life. Give yourself the gift of forgiveness today.

"I TRUST YOU"

Once we can genuinely say to ourselves, "I trust you", life as we know it will be forever changed. To be able to trust yourself means that you know beyond a shadow of a doubt that you will always do *right* by yourself. This is not to encourage selfish behavior and/or narcissism. This simply means that you have forgiven yourself, and love yourself enough to make the decisions in life that best benefit you. When you look into the mirror and say, "I trust you", you are saying to self: "I trust you to make the best decisions possible for you. I trust you not to abuse your body. I trust that you will not allow certain relationships into your life. I trust you to maintain a healthy thought life. I trust you to feed your soul and maintain a strong relationship with God. I trust you to be strong and stand up for yourself when necessary. Most importantly, I trust you enough to know that when you do make a mistake, you will love yourself enough to forgive and move forward." When we trust ourselves, we create a world of infinite possibilities.

Being able to trust yourself is a pre-requisite for building relationships with others. If you do not trust yourself, it is unlikely you will be able to genuinely trust anyone else. Your ability to trust your own judgment is not only essential for the building of personal relationships, but for every situation you will face in life. You have to get to a place where you know with utmost certainty that you can trust your own judgment. The absence of self-trust can be catastrophic. It can lead you into making decisions that were cultivated by fear versus confidence.

FORGIVE TODAY BECAUSE YOUR FUTURE DEPENDS ON IT.

The old saying, "past performance is indicative of future results" isn't always the truth. That saying may be applicable to those who are unaware of the power of God. However, for those who have a personal relationship with their Lord and Savior, you already know all things are possible. Jesus Christ makes the impossible quite possible. You are not defined by your past and as long as you have the courage to forgive, your past cannot hinder your future blessings from God. Regardless of your past, please know your future is as bright as you allow for it to be. By forgiving those who have harmed you, you are in essence telling God that even through your pain you are willing to be obedient.

Many of you may be asking yourselves, "How do I forgive? How do I begin the process of forgiveness when the offender has not yet apologized?" The first thing you need to know is that genuine forgiveness is not predicated on if you receive an apology or not. Even if the person who hurt you has not apologized, you are still able to forgive and move forward. You don't have to wait for an apology in order to set yourself free from the emotional bondage of unforgiveness. Waiting for an apology from the person or people who have wronged you is something you can choose to do. However, in doing so, you will only deepen the hurt and animosity felt toward the individual(s). In addition, you will unintentionally extend your emotional prison sentence. The uncomfortable truth is that while you remain resentful and overwhelmed with anger about what was done to you, it is highly likely the person/people who hurt you have moved on with their lives. The only one angry, hurting and losing sleep over the situation is you.

Don't allow your emotions to control you or in any way hinder your healing process. Let go of everything you've been holding onto and today, decide to give yourself the gift of freedom. Holding a grudge should be compared to that of refusing to toss a hand grenade. What you are holding is extremely powerful. If you refuse to let it go, it will inevitably cause destruction. Below are the basic steps you'll need to take to forgive someone who has hurt you.

1. *Make up your mind*. Do not waver back and forth about your decision to forgive. It must be a wholehearted decision that you make. Forgiveness is definitive.
2. *Continually seek God*. The act of forgiveness is truly divine. The complete act of forgiveness will always require help from the Almighty. Don't be foolish enough to believe this is something you can successfully do on your own. If that were the case, you would have done it already. Align your actions with the prayers you send forth for help in this area.
3. *Pray earnestly for the person who has hurt you*. As you cover them in prayer, God will work in their lives;

possibly providing them with a revelation that will yield an apology or better yet, changed behaviors.

4. *Make the commitment to forgive and refuse to pick up the grudge again*. Often times we *say* that we have forgiven and truly have the best of intentions. Yet the minute we are presented with an unfavorable situation, many of us pick that grudge back up and add onto it!

Forgiving people who have hurt you deeply is in no way an easy thing to do. In fact, it is often the most difficult and where many of us get caught up. My personal testimony is that forgiveness took over two years. The anger and bitterness I had toward the person who hurt me was unrelenting. It felt impossible to let go of the hurt and seemed like every time there was progression toward forgiveness, there would soon be significant setbacks. The real problem was my active mental archive of this person's wrong doing. There was too much focus on what had been done to hurt me and not enough focus on why it was important to let it all go.

FORGIVENESS IS NOT FOR THE OTHER PERSON; IT IS FOR YOU.

When you are at your lowest and the hurt is still incredibly real to you, it is difficult to fathom the possibility of forgiving. Everything in you wants the person to feel what you feel and know how their words or actions have affected you. Forgiving the person does not mean you are required to keep silent about the issues of your heart. There is nothing at all wrong with open communication (verbal or written) to express how you feel. However, after you have expressed how you feel, you must be willing to bring the situation to a close and forgive. In the words of Nelson Mandela, "As I walked out the door toward the gate that would lead to my freedom, I knew that if I didn't leave my bitterness and hatred behind, I'd still be in prison." No one can ever take away your ability to choose freedom from emotional bondage. The only person who has the power to do that is you. You have the option to sit and mentally rehearse all that has been done wrong to you. However, doing so will not change anything that has happened in the past; nor will it automatically generate a heartfelt apology from the person who wronged you. Be courageous and decide once and for all that the prison of unforgiveness is no longer where you want to reside. Life is for the living and you deserve to experience the fullness thereof. Your journey to restoration can go no further than you allow. Set yourself free!

Prayer:

Lord, forgive me. Please forgive me for the grudges I have held against others and myself. Help me to always understand that as a Christian, forgiving others is your expectation of me. I do not have the right to fall on bended knee and ask for your forgiveness and yet refuse to provide that same grace and mercy to others. I do not want to be a hypocrite any longer; expecting from you that which I am unwilling to give others. I understand that I am not exempt of betrayal and disappointment. Lord Jesus, you were hurt by those closest to you. You know deeply the pain and disappointment of betrayal. Help me to always keep in mind that these unsettling situations will happen in life but that will never justify the holding of a grudge. No matter how serious the offense, help me to always remember the power of forgiveness and the freedom that comes as a result. Amen!

CHAPTER 6: REFLECTIONS

Learning how to forgive yourself and others is an essential part of the restoration process. Take some time answer the following questions:

1. **After reading Chapter 6, how has your definition of forgiveness changed? If it hasn't, please explain.**

    _____

    _____

    _____

    _____

2. Are you a typically an unforgiving person? Do you hold grudges against yourself and others? Why or why not?

_____

_____

_____

_____

3. You *must* be willing to love, trust, and forgive <u>yourself</u> at all times. Complete the following:

I *love* you because:

_____

I *trust* you to:

_____

I forgive you for:

_____

CHAPTER 7: SEASON OF SELF (SOS)

The acronym SOS is the commonly used description for the international Morse code distress signal. It is a signal to express an immediate need for help. For the purposes of this chapter, "SOS" is an acronym for "Season of Self". Many of us have been moving throughout life at lightning speed. Now you've gotten to a place where it feels like everything has slowed down and you've gone as far as your human efforts will take you. At this very point in your life you are spiritually sending out an "SOS" distress signal and God's answer to you will be a Season of Self.

For everything there is indeed a set season. Many of us experience frustration because we don't know how to identify and accept the seasons we are in at any given time. The season you *want* to be in may not be the season you are actually in right now. The restoration process is not easy, but after you have let go of the past and forgiven the person who hurt you—you are now in a position to better understand and accept where you are in the present. Your 'Season of Self' is a major step in the restoration process. Right away you must understand there is no set time frame. You may be in this "season" for a significant stretch of time as every individual is different. During this distinct period you are getting to know God and in doing so, gaining a more profound definition of self. Many of us are extremely confident that we already have clear self-definition. Challenge yourself to consider the possibility that your current definition of self does not align favorably with God's definition of you.

The word of God implores us to understand that He knew us before we existed in the physical realm. Therefore, his knowledge of us is infinite. He knows things about you that you can only *hope* to be revealed in your lifetime. Your definition of self is limited to your finite life span and the result of life's circumstances, trials, and tribulations that have somehow molded you into who you are today. God sees you for the being that he created; absolute perfection. As you get closer to Him, he will indeed reveal who you are by *His* definition. However, He won't stop there. If you diligently seek the answers, He will both reveal and usher you into your purpose.

It is during this phase you will be most inquisitive. So far you have overcome many obstacles during the restoration process and are feeling confident. Your Season of Self is a time for discovery. In this season you are most likely to find out why the ending of your relationship happened, what you could have done differently, and what you can learn from this experience. When we know better, we can do better as a result of applying the information we've acquired from hard bought life lessons. However, when we know our*selves*, we can do even more!

"KNOWING YOURSELF IS THE BEGINNING OF ALL WISDOM." – ARISTOTLE

If many of you are honest, what you know most about yourself is that you rarely spend any time with yourself. Some of us are so afraid of being alone that we will forgo seeing a new movie, shopping in the mall, or enjoying a meal at a fantastic restaurant. We worry about how arriving alone will make us look in the eyes of others. Our fears are so fixated on the perception of being a "loner" or someone who "can't get a date", we would rather stay in the house and forgo new life experiences! As you go through your season of self, you will become more and more comfortable with who you are and what you like. God will also reveal to you the joy of solitude and the importance of knowing yourself before you seek to intimately know others.

Some people are so broken and hurt by past relationships and experiences that they've unknowingly gone into hiding. Hiding does not only mean you are locked in your house avoiding social activities or communication with others. That form of hiding is simply indicative of the fact that you are hiding from other people. It is equally possible to hide out in the open. The social events you attended on Monday, Wednesday, Friday, Saturday, and Sunday of last week left you feeling like quite the social butterfly. You are geared up to do it all over again this week. However, your social schedule leaves you with approximately two days out of the week to spend any significant amount of with yourself. If your schedule looks like this, it is highly likely you are hiding out in the open and you the person you are avoiding is *yourself*!

Your season of self will yield a new wave of maturity like you've never experienced. As you get to know yourself, you will be empowered to make the decisions that best serve you. You can't imagine it right now, but there will actually come a time when you will pass up an opportunity to go and hang out with friends because your inner man simply has a desire for a nice hot bath, soft music, and prayer. As you get to know yourself, you will also be more in tuned with what your spirit desires.

LIVE LIFE KNOWING GOD HAS HIS BEST FOR YOU!

Your prayer life will begin to explode as your relationship with God blossoms. And you will certainly need it. As with each step of the restoration process, faith is imperative here. It's actually quite possible that this is the stage in which your faith muscle will be most exercised. Again, you must keep in mind there is no set time for each Season of Self. You may be in this personal growth chamber for more time than you'd ever imagined. It is **faith** that will bring you through it and out on the other side completely restored. What you have to do at this time is make the commitment to yourself that regardless of how long this season is for you, you are determined to complete it.

In Ecclesiastes 3:1-8 we come to understand there is in fact a season for everything. A time to gain, a time to lose; A time to keep, a time to throw away; A time to weep and a time to laugh. Sometimes we want so desperately to be in a relationship when it is actually a season of consecration. It a season in which God wants you all to Himself so that he may correct and perfect you. You have to be willing to ask and be honest with yourself about what season of life you are currently in. Put aside your wants and desires for a moment and focus solely on your truth. Are you truly ready for a relationship right now? Are your finances in order? Are you satisfied with your career? Are you doing everything possible to prosper your spirit? Are you healthy both physically and emotionally? All the answers to these questions encompass the essence of *you*. If you are willing to do the hard work, you will come out on the other side stronger, and wiser than you've ever been before!

You are probably saying to yourself, "that's all sounds nice but how *long* is this 'season of self'?" Your season will be dependent upon how much work needs to be done and your willingness to submit to the process. Plainly put, the more you resist the longer it will take. God wants you to know genuine change does not happen overnight. It comes with hard work, diligence, and sacrifice. You didn't climb into the mess you are in overnight and unfortunately it will be the same slow moving process to get out of your current situation. However, the true benefit of a 'Season of Self' is acquired patience and a strengthened bond with your Lord and Savior. You will learn how to wait on and trust the Lord's timing for everything in your life. He will prove to you time and again that His timing and His plans for your life are far better than anything you could have dreamed or imagined on your own. You will learn that nothing you can do—no prayer, no amount of tears will force His hand to give you something for which He feels you are not yet ready.

Impatient people typically fall off during the 'Season of Self' because the flesh is pulling them back into a space of lust, desire, and instant gratification. We all want to be loved. We all want to be desired. We all want to matter to someone else. All of these things are indeed natural. However, during this 'Season of Self', you are being positioned to first love yourself, know yourself, and make yourself a priority. Only once you've accomplished these things can you genuinely press toward the possibility of sharing your life with someone else. Your 'Season of Self' will challenge you to make improvements in every area that is keeping you from living your best life.

Life has crippled you and circumstances have left you weakened. This period of time should be used to allow God to breathe life back into every area that has laid dormant. The sole purpose of this significant block of time is to allow God to restore and strengthen you again. He does this by revealing who you are and transforming you back into the person He originally created you to be, not what you've become as a result of the burdens of life.

GOD SAYS, "...AGAIN I WILL BUILD YOU AND YOU SHALL BE REBUILT." - JEREMIAH 31:3.

Your season of self is about coming to understand who you are, what experiences have contributed to your current state of mind, and what changes you need to make. During your SOS, there will be an unrelenting battle between your ego and God himself. As God reveals who we are, many of us have a natural inclination to either hide or adamantly defend our current behaviors. Many of us claim to prefer knowing the truth, but no one really enjoys being corrected. As you pray and ask God to reveal truths to you, be open minded and prepared for the possibility of sheer embarrassment as you come face to face with God's truth; not your own. It will not be easy to accept having all of your flaws on display. Yet, in order to rebuild there must be a period of deconstruction. During this season, God will work overtime to show you the areas in which you need immediate correction. It could be anything from laziness and procrastination to more serious offenses like foul language, or tendency to engage in violent behavior.

Although at times painful, your season of self will be an unbelievable blessing that will change your life forever. This period is intimate and to be enjoyed with your Creator. No one has to know that you are currently "under construction" or why. What you are experiencing can remain solely between you and your Creator if you choose. You cannot change that of which you are unaware. God will use various people and situations to prompt internal dialogue. You will start to ask yourself questions like, "Did I need to react that way?" or "was there something I could have done or said differently to yield a more favorable result?" Be open to the correction and know for sure God will not challenge you further than your capabilities. A demand for change in your life has brought you to this season. It is entirely up to you to make sure to get the most out of it at this time. You will never be in this space, at this time again and therefore you should view it for the unique opportunity it is!

Take the time to genuinely enjoy this season of change. In Romans 12:2 we are reminded to refrain from conforming to the world but being *transformed* by the renewing of our minds. The restoration process requires a stripping down to one's original state. Change is imperative and you should not expect to come out of this experience with the same mindset with which you began. As you get closer to God during this season and learn more about yourself you will begin to reject anything and anyone that does not agree with God's definition of you. You will begin to view yourself as regal, more than worthy of the best because you are in fact blessed by the best! This season will be an emotional roller coaster, but if you can get past the labor pains, you will indeed give birth to the promises God placed in you long before you came into existence. **You are worth it!**

Prayer:

Lord I thank you for this season and I accept that you are all-knowing. Your ways and thoughts are higher than mine and I am fully submitted to your correction. Teach me your ways and help me to be a reflection of you in all that I say and do. I am not used to being alone and this period of time feels very unnatural to me. Please minister to the part of me that is afraid of solitude. Help me to learn the importance of recharging my own life batteries by spending significant time in prayer and meditation. From day to day I interact with other people so much so that my own voice has started to be drowned out. I don't know where the thoughts and ideas of other people end and mines begin! Lord, I thank you for this period of time you have designed just for me. I am grateful for the opportunity to get to learn things about myself that I never knew before. I know this time in my life may not be the easiest, but your word promises to complete the work you've started in me. Please cleanse me of any pride or ego that would in any way hinder my ability to hear from you. I thank you in advance for your unconditional (Agape) love as I go through the highs and lows of this season. I know this season will be difficult and full of challenges, but in the end it will be worth it and I will never be the same again! Amen.

CHAPTER 7: REFLECTIONS

Your Season of Self will be the perfect opportunity for you to learn things about yourself that you never knew!

1. This extremely important 'season' will be key to your overall personal transformation. Do you currently carve out time each day for yourself? If not, what *really* keeps you from spending quality time alone?

    _____

    _____

    _____

    _____

2. Are you prepared to learn things about yourself that may be highly unfavorable and in need of immediate change? How do you typically handle "correction" of any kind?

    _____

    _____

    _____

    _____

3. How would you describe your current relationship with
    God? If it is not as strong as you would like it to be,
    what are you doing to change that?

    _____

    _____

    _____

    _____

CHAPTER 8: WHAT ABOUT YOUR FRIENDS?

As you continue to move along throughout this experience it is important that you allow yourself to be keenly aware of your surroundings. Everything going on inside of you is equally important to what is taking place on the outside. There will come a point in the process where you will be forced to closely analyze the company you are keeping. Your successful completion of the restoration process will depend heavily upon your diligence in this particular area.

Friendship is often a complicated topic to discuss because everyone has a different definition of what having a friend and being a friend entails. So for the sake of clarity, when friendship is mentioned in this text, you are at liberty to incorporate your very own definition of what friendship means to you. In fact, you are highly encouraged to take this time out to define or redefine what friendship means to you. Based on your definition, you will be empowered to move forward and make solid decisions as needed.

Jim Rohn was quoted as saying, "You are the average of the five people you spend the most time with." What do those words mean to you? As you continue through this process and seek full restoration in your life, expect change. You must be open the possibility of some immediate changes to your current inner circle. In order for this experience to be successful, you will need to have the right people by your side. It is really just that simple. There is nothing that can potentially get you off track faster, than to be surrounded by people whose relationships are in no way beneficial to you.

"NO MAN IS AN ISLAND" –JOHN DONNE

As human beings we are in need of interaction with other people from all walks of life. Trying to live our lives separated from others, and void of association is preposterous. We were created to engage and learn as much as possible from each other. We should always be open to finding and nurturing alliances with other people. However, the key is to foster and maintain friendships that are prospering to you mind, body, and soul.

We all need a solid support system in our lives. The Bible (NIV) reminds us in Proverbs 18:24 that "One who has unreliable friends soon comes to ruin, but there is a friend who sticks closer than a brother." It is a marvel that although written over 2000 years ago, the Word of God is alive and still provides us guidance and counsel even today. This scripture is extremely important to understand as you press toward your goal of restoration. On one hand, the word is telling us that unreliable friends will be your downfall. Truth be told, we can stop right there and look no further. God's Word is telling us that we need to be careful about the people we have around us! The scripture also then goes on to tell you that there is a friend who will be closer to you than your own blood.

If we are honest with ourselves, many of us may absolutely have a friend that knows more about our darkest secrets and life experiences than a blood relative. For whatever reason, this friend is a kindred spirit and there is a strong, beautiful bond between the two of you. This individual has proven to be both loyal and consistent through good times and bad. You trust this person with your life and never question his/her intentions where you are concerned. This friendship is a gift to you and on many days you don't know what you'd do without it. God smiles upon friendship, and it is His desire that you always be connected to the *right* people.

Your inner circle of friends are those people who satisfy your need for a more profound intimate, emotional connection. Typically, there are not many members of your inner circle. These are the friends you trust with your deepest secrets. These are the friends who treat your children like theirs. These are the friends who are there when you need them; anticipating your needs and are already on task before you can ask. These are the friends whose patience with you never seems to run out; your flaws aren't flaws at all to them. These are the friends who not only allow you to be yourself, but encourage authenticity. Make no mistake about it, friendships within your inner circle are not exempt from disagreements. However, even the disagreements you have within this circle of friends will serve to strengthen the bond. There is a genuine affinity and love shared with the people of your inner circle. The trademarks of inner-circle friendships are trust, loyalty, and maturity. All of these things will consistently work together to enrich the profoundness of the relationships. The people within your inner circle must edify you. Jealousy and/or envy doesn't exist within your inner circle because these people genuinely want to see you prosper and live your best life.

While we would love to constantly be surrounded by these types of people, the reality is that not many of them exist. An inner circle friendship will take time to grow. It will endure many seasons of change; not all favorable. But in the end you will come to recognize it as the solid foundation and gifting in your life that God created it to be. The joy and peace of having a true friend is invaluable.

The outer circle of friends is also valuable, but there some distinct differences. This is the friend that you enjoy being around. This person is genuinely delightful and you share a few common interests. Your similar tastes in music are the catalyst behind next Saturday night's meet-up at the local jazz lounge. Your similar taste in Thai cuisine is the reason for Thursday's impromptu dinner after work. This friend is perfect to hang out with or talk to on the phone for hours recapping the latest episode of your favorite television series. However, when disaster strikes and you are in need of help, this person typically does not come to mind. While there are no hard feelings about it, you are simply not expecting this outer circle friend to be there for you in any profound capacity. If you pay close attention to these types of friendships, you'll notice the conversation is never too deep or meaningful; very surface level. You share information, but it's nothing too serious or incriminating. The reason for this is because although you like this person, you haven't yet established the mutual trust required to expose yourself. The friendships of the outer circle lack the breadth and depth of those within the inner circle.

Interestingly enough, often times the outer circle of friends were once part of your inner circle. Perhaps time, marriage, children, a career move to a different state, or just life in general changed the dynamic of the friendship. Sometimes even the closest friends will drift apart as they mature and navigate throughout life. More than likely, at least one of the people in your outer circle of friends is someone you've known for a relatively long period of time. You haven't broken off the friendship completely because technically this person hasn't done anything to warrant such a drastic decision. Your choice to maintain the friendship is more out of loyalty to the length of time you've known the person than to the actual quality of the current relationship.

THE UNIVERSAL RULE FOR FRIENDSHIP SHOULD ALWAYS BE QUALITY OVER QUANTITY.

Be very careful that whether part of your inner or outer circle, you are not keeping any people around you solely because of the length of time you have known them. The fact that you've known the person for twenty years is impressive. However, when you are in desperate need, it will be the quality of the friendship that gets you through difficult times, not how long you've known the person. It is perfectly acceptable to have someone in your inner circle that you've only known for a couple of years while your outer circle consists of someone you may have known all of your life. Your friendships must be defined by the quality of the relationships you have with them.

Many people make the mistake of confusing the members of their inner and outer circle. Take the time to create your list and be ready to make changes as needed. Do not be surprised at all if now that you've defined or redefined what friendship means to you, there are drastic changes. Be prepared for the possibility your list has not only been shortened, but there has been movement from the inner to the outer circle. In some cases, there will be movement from the outer circle to the far recesses of your mind. There doesn't need to a profound or significant reasoning behind these redefinitions of your relationships. It is as simple as defining what friendship means and following through to ensure your relationships are reflective of that particular definition.

Refrain from beating yourself up about the changes you are making in your life. These changes are extremely important and will only serve to benefit you in the future. This journey is not one-dimensional. Your complete restoration process will require you to analyze every aspect of your life. You must have the courage to make the difficult decision to let any/all relationships go that are no longer serving you. Do not allow the words of people or any guilt you may feel to initiate a change of mind once you are sure who should have limited access to you. You are *not* being judgmental by taking the necessary steps to separate yourself from people who are not headed in the same direction. This does not mean you love or respect them any less. You are simply acknowledging the power and direct influence of your surroundings. It is simply your choice be around those who are living positively.

Now that you have redefined what friendship means as well as made changes to your inner/outer circle, you can continue to press forward on the right track. In order to ensure the right people surround you, you must be committed to consistent assessment of your closest relationships. This shouldn't be something you do every 5 years; if you get around to do it at all. Your overall success in life is highly contingent upon the influences you are under. You are indeed a product of your environment. If your environment consists of toxic people, then you need to make changes or you will find yourself in trouble.

What does **toxic** mean? According to Webster's dictionary, there are multiple definitions of the word toxic.

1. Containing or being poisonous material especially when capable of causing death or serious debilitation.
2. Extremely harsh, malicious, or harmful
3. Relating to or being an asset that has lost so much value that it cannot be sold on the market

We often identify most with the first definition of the word toxic. When we hear "toxic" we think of poisonous material that could somehow cause death or harm; a danger to our physical bodies. Fortunately, most toxic materials are readily identifiable with some type of HAZMAT labeling. When you see those labels, you know right away to proceed with caution. For the purpose of this chapter, the toxicity we need to be mindful of in relationships is a form of danger to our emotional and spiritual being. What do you do about the toxic friendship that is not nearly as obvious to identify because there is no label attached? Let's review some of the different "types" of toxic friends:

THE PESSIMIST: This is the wonderful friend who always has something negative to say. You've proclaimed, "It's supposed to be 75 degrees today! I'm looking forward to the beautiful weather!" His/her reply is, "Yeah, but it's supposed to rain by tomorrow afternoon." This type of person always borrows from today's happiness to fulfill tomorrow's worry. If you ever bring it to their attention, this type of person will typically hide under the umbrella of, "I just keep it real". The worst part is that the pessimism often comes on the wings of "concern". For example: You've recently met someone new and call this friend to dish! As you tell your friend all about this new person in your life, filled with excitement, you wait for his/her feedback. More than likely, you'll receive a response along the lines of, "I'm happy for you! Just be careful though...you remember what happened last time..." In essence, what this person is doing is projecting negative energy onto you and your life situations. Be very careful about with whom you share knowledge of your blessings! On a personal level, this individual may be loyal, trustworthy, and everything you've ever wanted in a friend. It may be extremely hard for you to consider ending the friendship or limiting your time around him/her. However, what you must remember is that negativity is contagious. Eventually you will start to think and sound like this person because you are constantly exposed to their "stinking" thinking.

THE "YES" MAN: This is the individual that will agree with absolutely everything you say and/or do. You can do no wrong in this person's eyes. This type of friend is extremely uncomfortable with correcting you or offering any advice that opposes your view. The "yes" man (or woman) is a real problem. Just for the sake of maintaining a relationship void of conflict, this type of "friend" will not only watch you head in the wrong direction, but agree with you completely while you do it. These are one of the worst types of people to *knowingly* keep in your inner or outer circle. With determination and confidence, you can handle a pessimist quite easily. However, being consistently surrounded by someone who is unwilling to disagree with you to the point of potentially watching you fail is problematic. Proverbs 27:17 reads: "As iron sharpens iron, so one man sharpens another." This scripture reminds us of the importance of sharpening each other with truth. We sometimes forfeit significant life lessons for ourselves and others by refusing to say what we really think or feel. Seek to be around people who are honest, fearless, and will not hesitate to lovingly correct you when you are in need. The "yes" man may genuinely *care* for you, but he/she hasn't yet mastered the true meaning of friendship. A true friend will go beyond the care they have for you and provide tough love when necessary.

THE COMPLAINER: This type of friend cannot see the happiness or value in anything and therefore always find a reason to complain. Their faith is small (if existent at all) and they lack the ability to find the positive in any given situation. The Word of God reminds us in Philippians 2:14 to do everything without grumbling or arguing. We are imperfect beings and all of us have and will complain in our lifetime. However, having a close relationship with a chronic complainer will adversely affect your restoration process. These types of people do not genuinely understand the power of gratitude. They have not yet come to understand that in order to have more, we need to recognize and appreciate all that we currently have! The truth is, as you continue to go through your restoration process, you will see that this type of relationship will run its course naturally. As you are restored, your mind will change. You will no longer want to be surrounded by anything or anyone that even slightly emits negativity, brokenness, or bitterness.

THE SILENT COMPETITOR: It doesn't matter who you are, who your friends are, how long you've known them, or how good they've been to you. There is a silent competitor somewhere nearby. This person is at war with you in their own mind. It is their life's mission to "one-up" you any opportunity they get. This person only has the capacity to be *somewhat* happy for you when great things are happening in your life. The reason is because on one hand, they are genuinely glad something good happened to someone they consider a friend. On the other hand the happiness they feel for your shower of blessings is short-lived because immediately thereafter they are taxing their brains trying to figure out how to do better than you. This type of "friend" doesn't necessarily want you to be unhappy. He/she just doesn't want to see you happier than them. The silent competitor is in no way harmful to your restoration process per se. Simply put, this friendship is not mutually influential. The competitor is far more influenced by you and your lifestyle than you are by them. Even still, this type of friendship will in no way benefit you. This type of person is far too interested in their own needs and wants to be concerned with yours. Ultimately you will simply have to make a decision whether you want this type of person in your inner or outer circle.

THE EMOTIONAL DRAINER: You'll hear most from this type of friend when disaster strikes. Without knowing it, you've become his/her personal therapist. When all is well and wonderful things are happening in their lives, you aren't included. This is the type of friendship that can last for years because more than likely you are unaware that you are being used emotionally. You quite enjoy hearing from this friend (who is otherwise a great person) and providing sound advice to help alleviate any issues they are experiencing. You haven't yet arrived at the conclusion that you are being used for your positive energy. More than likely when *you* are in need, the 'Emotional Drainer' is nowhere to be found. He/she is busy living life to the fullest after accurately implementing the advice you've given so freely. Ralph Waldo Emerson said it best: in order to have a friend, you have to be one. This type of relationship is threatening to your restoration process because this type of friend will extract both your time and energy. There is no reciprocity whatsoever to be found here and this friendship is extremely parasitic.

THE FRENEMY: Highly likely to be in your inner circle, this person is someone you consider to be one of your very closest friends. The trust you two share is unprecedented. This individual is a solid support system, there for you whenever you need him/her, and never hesitates to offer words of encouragement when things are going wrong in your life. However, when things are going well, don't be surprised if you can't find this person in the daytime with a flashlight. This type of friend will absolutely be there for you. However, this friend is extremely supportive as long as your life is a mess and things are out of control. The minute you get your breakthrough, miracles begin to explode in your life, and unprecedented experiences start happening, they will be "busy" and unavailable to you. More than likely your friendship was born at a time when the two of you were in the same space emotionally, mentally, and/or spiritually. Over time this person has decided you are inferior to them -- not at all on their level. Any positive momentum in your life will trigger their insecurities and adversely affect this type of friendship. This type of toxicity in your life must be removed immediately.

THE WILD CHILD: This person is the life of the party. There is never a dull moment around this individual! You smile when you think about this friend because more than likely loyalty is what first comes to mind. He/she is your secret keeper, your road dog, and the person you know for certain will stand with you regardless of what comes your way. The problem here is that this type of friend is a loose cannon. You can't ever seem to be certain what the day will bring when dealing with him/her. What started out as a simple, fun-filled birthday celebration ended up with violence, handcuffs, someone riding in the backseat of a police car, and bail money. This friend is out of control and while you absolutely love him/her for their honesty, the mouths and fiery tempers on these types always lead to trouble. More than likely this friendship blossomed in your days of youth. Although one of the most loyal friends you have, this type of person could (although unintentionally) put you in a very compromising position. As you continue throughout your restoration process you will undoubtedly formulate a new definition of self. You will learn to accept who you are, where you are headed, and why certain people no longer fit into that equation. God warns us in Corinthians 15:33, "Do not be deceived. Bad company ruins good morals." This may not be a friend from whom you are ready to completely separate. Loyalty is not an easy trait to come by these days. However, you may need to proceed with caution. Your future is exceptionally bright and you cannot afford to be in bad company.

THE SUPERSTAR: This friend is good looking, brilliant, self-absorbed, but has the lowest self- esteem known to man. You are not a friend to this type of person; instead you are a "fan". Your role is to constantly sing this person's praises. If you aren't consistently telling them how fantastic they are, he/she will want very little to do with you. More than likely this person can be found in your outer circle. The relationship between the two of you would never be close enough for inner circle qualification. This individual displays a false humility, is most concerned with superficiality, and as a result there is often no depth of personality to explore. This type of friendship doesn't adversely affect you in any way other than being a complete waste of precious, invaluable time. As you seek God and get to know yourself on a level never before experienced, you honestly don't have the time to entertain those who only seek to use your positive energy to feed their starving egos.

THE JUDAS: Friendships can indeed be a beautiful gift from God. However, it will be impossible to make it through a lifetime of friendships without coming face to face with your own personal "Judas". This person is within your inner circle and therefore has an extensive knowledge of you. This knowledge includes past mistakes, present situations, and future aspirations. There is nothing you wouldn't share with this type of friend because this relationship was built on the foundation of a mutual trust that has never been compromised. The problem here is that the 'Judas' is often not readily identified before they strike. In the blink of an eye, the person closest to you can do something to betray the trust you've mutually established over time. This type of friend is someone close to you who will not hesitate to betray you at the first opportunity for self-promotion or advancement. The reason why this type of friend is so lethal is because knowledge is powerful. There is no limit to the information this person has of you. There is also no limit to the information they will divulge if they anticipate some type of personal benefit. Even still, you must not despise your 'Judas experience'. It will indeed be hurtful, but if you use the experience as God intended you will rise from the ashes like a Phoenix, stronger and more mature than ever.

PURPOSE-FILLED PEOPLE MUST BE SURROUNDED BY OTHER PURPOSE-FILLED PEOPLE.

There are a variety of friend "types" and by no means have all of them been listed. It is your responsibility to take the time to assess each of your friends. Defining your friendships isn't just about getting rid of relationships that are no longer mutually beneficial. It is also about learning how to interact and effectively communicate with those friends you've decided to keep in your life. As you continue to go throughout the restoration process you will notice a host of personal changes happening. Your mindset will be different and people you were once close to may become distant strangers. Do not be afraid of these inevitable changes that are going to take place. Accept that there are simply some friendships that have run their course.

As time goes by you will learn more about who you are, who God created you to be, and why certain experiences have happened in your life. The purpose of this restoration process is to take you to another level; heights unknown. It will become more evident why certain friendships are still intact while others have fallen by the wayside. Don't view an ended friendship as something negative. God knows for certain who needs to be in your life at any given time and who is serving as a barrier between you and your divine purpose.

Prayer:

Lord, I am in need of discernment. Please grant me the wisdom to be able to accurately assess my current friendships. This is an incredibly exciting time in my personal life and there are so many changes happening on the inside. Help me to understand that my external surroundings are a key component to my restoration as well. It is frightening to think about possibly losing some of the people closest to me. I have known many of my friends for years and we've been through a lot together. Faith is the absence of fear and I ask that you help me to make the right decisions where my relationships are concerned. For all of the friendships that must come to an end as a result of my obedience to you, please replace them with the right people. Your word reminds me that your plans and thoughts are higher than mine. I know you would not ask me to give up a friendship without replacing it with another far more amazing than the first. You know what you have purposed me to do in this life. Most of all, you know what relationships need to be formed and which need to be severed in order to remain in accordance with that purpose. Lord, I trust you and thank you in advance for a new definition of friendship and circle of friends that are indeed truly a blessing to me. Amen!

CHAPTER 8: REFLECTIONS

Your immediate surroundings are also a very important key to complete restoration. The company you keep is essential! Take some time to reflect on what you've just read in Chapter 8 and answer the questions below.

1. Write down the names of your closest friends. See if you are able to identify any of the "types" within your inner/outer circle.

_____

_____

_____

_____

_____

_____

_____

_____

2. Everyone has experienced the sting of a "Judas". What valuable lessons did you learn from that situation?

_____

_____

_____

_____

3. Do you currently have "friendships" that are no longer serving you? Are you willing to sever any/all relationships lacking mutual benefit?

_____

_____

_____

_____

_____

CHAPTER 9: ALL THINGS IN ORDER

Many will make the inaccurate assumption that your journey to restoration is solely about repairing a broken heart and getting your love life back on track. In actuality, this intense process will encompass every aspect of your life. What would be the point of healing only a broken heart when there are so many other components of your life that are broken? 1 Corinthians 14:40 reads, "But all things should be done decently and in order". Before you can move forward from where you are right now, you will have to ensure every part of self is in order. Without a desire to identify areas that need change and the determination to follow through, a complete restoration process is not possible.

This chapter was written to encourage you to take a closer look at your whole being: **MIND, BODY,** and **SOUL**. As we go throughout life we get into our daily routines and more often than not, one or more of those areas will suffer greatly. God's word encourages us to remember the importance of balance; no one area is more important than the other. In fact, all three of those components are very much interdependent and need to be equally exercised to maintain the best "you".

MIND

The brain is an incredibly complex machine. It is impossible to know even a small percentage of how it works and not be in complete awe. The mind is incredibly powerful and therefore must be protected at all times. When the enemy wants to get you off track, it will all start with a thought. Your thoughts will then lead to actions, and your actions will always yield a reaction. While going through your restoration process it is important you are empowered with the knowledge that your mind will inevitably be under attack. Peace of mind is just about the last thing your spiritual adversary wants you to have. There will be seasons in your life where trouble may seem to lurk on every side. To be candid with you, your restoration process will at times feel extremely grueling. There *will* be torrential downpours before you can bask in the sunshine.

The most effective way to keep your mind at peace is to prohibit the development of negative thought patterns. Negative self-talk, (often originated from low self-esteem) will adversely affect your peace of mind. Learn how to train your mind to think positively. When negative thoughts pop into your mind, fight back immediately by counteracting that thought with something positive. Don't subscribe to negative thoughts because they will encourage you to consider regressing and going back to old habits that feel safest. American writer, columnist and playwright George Ade once said, "familiarity breeds contentment". The mind is powerful and you are going to have to work considerably hard to avoid reverting back to your familiar ways. Train your mind to accept that you are striving to attain "next level" living. As you are being restored, you should be seeking to soak up everything new around you. Your past mindset supported past behaviors, which led to past results. If you genuinely desire a forward shift in your life, a new way of thinking and living is essential.

In addition, a negative mindset can help to initiate the ongoing comparison of yourself to others. You become more focused on what other people are doing in their lives than your own. This is the most successful way to sidetrack your own restoration process and feed into negative self-talk.

It is important to carve out time to clear your mind, meditate on God's grace, and stay in a space of gratefulness. You must always endeavor to remember where God has brought you come from. What experiences in your life did you think would ruin you and yet you are here to talk about them? Keep an ongoing log of your own personal testimonies. Just when you are all geared up to send out invitations to your pity party, review your list of triumphs instead. God has been more gracious to you than you could ever deserve. Keep your mind focused on all of the things that you have because of His mercy. Spend absolutely no time worrying about what you cannot control.

REAL, EFFECTIVE CHANGE FIRST HAPPENS IN THE MIND.

The most important change that will happen during this process is the renewing of your mind. There must be a genuine paradigm shift in order for change to take place. This is why the devil doesn't want you to think differently or change your mind about certain areas in your life. If your paradigm can remain the same, then you will continue to do, say, and engage in all of the things you used to. You made up in your mind you wanted that Master's degree and then you attained it. You made up in your mind that you were tired of renting and wanted to purchase your first home, then you did it. You made up in your mind that you wanted to lose 20 pounds by the New Year and you did it. All of what you are going to accomplish in this life is going to first originate in your mind. That is the exact same way for all of the bad decisions you've made. They all started in your mind. Your complete restoration will yield a new way of thinking. By thinking differently, your actions will also change. This is the beginning of a new life for you!

A new, improved mindset will attract someone who is in a similar head-space. The "type" of significant other you used to find appealing will no longer be attractive or attracted to you. You will start to grab the attention of different types of people. The reason for this is because you are on a different wavelength. The caliber of people you used to be attracted to will no longer speak to the essence of new "you". Likewise, you will not appeal to those who can't understand the new level of thinking you've acquired.

BODY

1 Corinthians 6: 19-20 reads, "Do you not know that your bodies are temples of the Holy Spirit, who is in you, whom you have received from God? You are not your own; you were bought at a price. Therefore honor God with your bodies." Your body is God's temple. It is the resting place of the Holy Spirit. Many of us forget that important fact as we go throughout our everyday lives.

Before you read any further, it is important for you to understand this section is not about narcissism or vanity. Our bodies are the vessels we've been given to carry out our divine assignments throughout life. If there is one thing a billionaire currently battling a terminal illness can tell you, it would be that health truly is wealth. He/she would give any amount of money to be able to "buy" a cure for the health crisis with which they are currently contending. Without health, nothing else is possible. It is your responsibility to ensure you are making healthy decisions that will enhance your life. How would you describe your current diet? What physical activities are you engaging in on a regular basis? Do you refrain from smoking and/or excessively drinking alcohol? These are highly important questions that need your consideration.

There are many aspects of life that we cannot control. However, our overall health is not one of them. We are empowered with extensive health information from doctors, magazines, journals, etc. to take control of our lives. Our health is something that we can proactively contribute to making better. Committing to a healthy lifestyle helps to ensure that you are doing your part to maintain good health. Does going to the gym every day and eating right mean you will never face a health crisis? Unfortunately, that is not how life works. However, there are diseases that doctors have confirmed are in direct correlation to unhealthy eating habits, drinking, smoking, and living a sedentary lifestyle. What are you willing to do in order to make sure your body is in its best shape possible? Again, this is not about maintaining a certain figure to attract others. By taking care of your body you show respect for the temple God created and in doing so, engage in practices that display **self-love**.

Often times we have a lengthy list of physical requirements for the mate of our dreams. The first question you should ask yourself is if everything you desire of your mate in physical appearance is something that you bring to the table. Is it really fair to require your mate be physically fit and healthy when you are overweight, unhealthy and have been paying on a gym membership but haven't worked out over 8 months?

Along with looking good comes feeling good. When you feel good about yourself, your decision-making is on point and you are no longer reacting from a place of low self-esteem, desperation or fear. When you feel good about yourself on the inside and out, there is an air of newness that engulfs you. In your mind, possibilities are limitless and there is nothing that can stop you from living your best life.

Your beauty and self-acceptance should radiate from the inside. The latest styles and fashions can never erase the truth about how you feel about yourself. Material things may help to mask various issues, but the success of your restoration depends on your ability to acknowledge past issues, get closure, and bury them once and for all. For those who may be dealing with body image issues, there must be a willingness to once and for all confront your individual situations. With hard work and determination, you can finally learn to deal with whatever issues are driving you to harm your body by overeating, smoking, drinking, denying yourself proper nutrition, and/or living an excessively sedentary lifestyle.

Poet William Shakespeare once said, "Self-love, my liege, is not so vile a sin as self-neglecting." Until you have completely fallen in love with all of the uniqueness that works together to create the amazing individual that you are, there should no expectation for others to do so. Many believe they are capable of masking low self-esteem, however it is important for you to know that is impossible. Some may have perfected the ability to cover their issues with the best in brand named clothing, fancy cars, and other material things. Yet, even if they have managed to cover how they really feel about themselves through self-presentation, the low esteem of self is still identifiable. You can put a dress on an elephant, but it is still an elephant. Your outer person may look amazingly beautiful. However, your low self-esteem will be revealed in the things you say (don't say) or things you do (don't do). Make your health and wellness a non-negotiable priority from this day forward. Being healthy is not about attracting a certain caliber of mate. Rather, it is about living long enough to experience the fullness of life God intended for you!

SOUL

This entire chapter was designed to illustrate the importance of having all things in order. We've already discussed the importance of keeping both the mind and body in order. While they are all of equal importance in the earthly realm, there is one last aspect of life to consider and it could possibly be most important because it is everlasting. When we leave the earthly realm, our bodies and the minds inside them will turn to the dust from which it was created. Our souls will last for an eternity and it is imperative we operate from day to day recognizing the importance of consistently keeping our souls in order. John talks about the prosperity of the soul in 3 John 1:2 (NKJV). He writes *"Beloved, I pray that you may prosper in all things and be in health, just as your soul prospers."* From that scripture we are able to understand that good health and overall prosperity is closely linked to the prosperity of the soul. We come to understand that John believed the prospering of one's soul was just as important as every other aspect of an individual's life.

The Merriam-Webster's dictionary has defined the 'soul' as:

1. the immaterial essence, animating principle, or actuating cause of an individual life
2. the spiritual principle embodied in human beings, all rational and spiritual beings, or the universe
3. a person's total self

Your soul is the immortal essence of you. It is the part of you that can and will never cease to exist. Our souls are incredibly important but sadly, we tend to spend so little time engaging in activities that will offer the sustenance it needs to thrive. There are many ways we can proactively feed and nurture our souls. As you continue throughout your restoration journey, the growth and prospering of your soul will be inevitable. In fact, you will find your soul yearning and longing for growth and development. It is your responsibility to answer the call and seek new levels of understanding in your spirituality.

The first, most important way to begin to prosper your soul is through prayer. Prayer is simply communication between you and God. Your prayers do not have to be fancy and full of articulate verbiage. The only requirement for prayer is that it be open, honest, and done as often as possible. Yes! Prayer can be done anywhere and at any time. It is an extremely powerful method of communication with God and in order to keep that power activated consistently in your life, you must be committed to doing it often. The beautiful thing about prayer is that there is no topic off limits. Learn to pray and communicate consistently with your Lord and Savior with the same excitement and candor as you do your best friends. Do not allow any issues or circumstances to frustrate, worry, or frighten you so badly that there is an adverse effect on your prayer life. When your prayer life is intact, everything else *has* to follow.

As a Christian, it is your responsibility to do everything you can to prosper your own soul. However, God has ordained chosen men and women of God to cover you in prayer, counsel you, and guide you in the earthly realm. If you are not part of the church, then you are lacking an important covering system. Each Sunday morning you should be intentionally feeding your soul with a powerful message from a man or woman of God.

In addition, a church home will surround you with people who are seeking God's guidance just like you. A church is a great way to socialize and make new circles of friends who are like-minded. A church home is also a great place to find mentorship, counseling, and most of all develop your personal ministry of service. We were all created to serve in some capacity while in the earthly realm. Being involved in church is a great way to explore what your gifts are and how best to utilize them. Attending church regularly should be less about fulfilling some type of obligation and more about feeding a soul that is hungry and in desperate need of nourishment.

Another way to prosper your soul is to give and serve. If in fact the goal is for your soul to resemble Jesus Christ, then you are a servant. Regardless of what your checking and savings account says, you are a servant. Regardless of the car you currently drive and/or home you live in, you are a servant. As you help and serve others, you are making deposits of love, faith, and hope. As you prosper others, you prosper your own soul. There are so many who truly don't understand the concept of giving. In today's society there is such emphasis on competition. Many are overwhelmingly concerned with outrunning, outwitting, and outlasting their neighbor. As Christians we should know better than anyone else that we are our brother's keeper. You have a distinct assignment to help as many people as you possibly can while here on earth. As you give by releasing time and resources to others, you are actually storing up your own blessings!

Service does not always have to be on a grand scale. There are many people who may be unable to give monetary donations to community fundraisers or non-profit organizations. Time is far more valuable currency. Call your local soup kitchen and volunteer for a shift to help cook or clean. Research some local non-profit organization and see if there is a need for any skill sets you may be able to offer. Knock on the door and offer a home cooked meal to your elderly neighbor. Mentor or tutor a young child in the community that is struggling in a particular subject. Instead of throwing money in a tin can and continuing along your way, sit down next to the homeless man or woman and offer a listening ear. Pray with him/her and share the good news of hope, joy, and peace that you've been offered as a Christian. There are so many creative ways for you to serve others without the need of money.

No one promised this journey would be an easy one for you. However, your restoration process will be an emotional, spiritual, and physical transformation that will forever change your life. Open your mind and make a wholehearted commitment to maintaining a healthy balance of mind, body, and soul!

Prayer:

Thank you for your Word that reminds me of the importance of maintaining decency and order in my life. Right now there may be an imbalance but I am certain that with your help in conjunction with my steadfast efforts in these areas, there is nothing that I can't accomplish! Lord, I commit my mind to you right now. Help me to take control of my thought life and learn how to cease all negative thoughts that try to hinder me. I am committed to remaining on a frequency of gratitude. I understand my responsibility to upkeep the vessel you've created in your likeness and image. I am fully committed to a healthy, active lifestyle that will help me to live my best life. Finally, Lord I thank you for the desire to prosper my soul. I thank you for my current or future church home. Thank you for the new relationships that I will make as a result of being part of the church community. I am excited about the changes on the horizon and thank you for each and every experience! Amen!

CHAPTER 9: REFLECTIONS

Complete restoration will involve the transformation of your mind, body, and soul. Use the questions below to help you assess where you are in these areas of your life.

1. MIND: What activities to you currently engage in that contribute to the edification of your mind?

_____

_____

_____

_____

_____

2. **BODY:** Are you actively participating in a lifestyle that includes physical activity and healthy eating habits? If not, what changes are you willing to make? Why are those changes important?

_____

_____

_____

_____

_____

3. **SOUL:** Do you currently have a church home? If so, are you an active member? If not, what steps are you taking to find one? How would you describe your current prayer life?

_____

_____

_____

_____

_____

CHAPTER 10: TIMEKEEPER

P eople tend to pay very close attention and make ongoing assessments of how much money they have to spend, invest, and/or donate. However, for some strange reason we don't view our **time** the same way. As a result of our inability to be more intentional about time, we often waste an incredibly valuable resource. The first thing you must know for sure is that time is much more valuable than any currency known to man. There is a wealthy billionaire walking this earth who has learned that even the extent of his/her money cannot buy time.

TIME IS THE GREAT EQUALIZER.

Each day is filled with 24 hours and no one person has more time to use than another. The President, pro-athletes, police officers, teachers and preachers are all given the same 24 hours in a day to utilize. The total amount of hours, minutes, and seconds are all the very same. If that is the case, why are our lives all so very different? Why are some able to use their 24 hours to make great contributions to society while others are not? The answer is as simple as time *management.* To manage something is to have control over or handle with a certain degree of skill. How well do you manage your time?

People that have experienced major accomplishments over their life span, put forth significant effort to manage their time. They have mastered the ability to not only set goals, but to use time as a resource instead of a hindrance -- filled with purpose, intention, and hard work. On the contrary, there is always a group of people who will look at the accomplishments of others in awe; truly unable to understand how these great tasks were accomplished. They often pacify themselves with excuses that sound like, "I could have done that if only I had the time", and "I had that idea, but I am so busy." An idea will always be *just* an idea without any action behind it. It can never materialize into anything significant if there is no activity that will bring it to life. There are only so many hours in a day, none of which can be reclaimed. Whatever the details of your personal definition of time, it can't be stored, saved or borrowed. Once it's gone, it's gone.

Time is a gift and although it would seem unfair, everyone is not given the same amount of time to carry out their purpose here on earth. Time is relative and it is important to consider the concept of time from your Creator's perspective. We currently reside in the physical realm and recognize time to be something that is finite. Seconds, minutes, hours, days, and years are what we use to help provide a mental construct of time. However, God dwells in a different dimension otherwise known as the spirit realm. That realm is beyond the perception of our physical senses. God is not limited to the physical laws and dimensions of time we have come to know as human beings.

In Psalm 90:4, we are able to read a description of the timelessness of God. "For a thousand years in Your sight are like a day that has just gone by, or like a watch in the night." In this short scripture you can see the infinite definition of time as seen by God being contrasted from the finite classification understood by man.

While time is extremely important to us in the physical realm, please understand the passing of time is irrelevant to God because He transcends it.

In 2 Peter 3:8, we are admonished not to be confused about the concept of time. We are lovingly reminded that God's perspective of time is completely different from mankind. The scripture reads, "But do not forget this one thing, dear friends: With the Lord a day is like a thousand years, and a thousand years like a day." The Lord will never view time as we do. We are only physically here for a set amount of time while God is an everlasting spirit. God sees all of eternity and the time that passes on earth is of no significance from His eternal perspective.

There is no way possible for us to truly understand the idea of eternity or the endlessness of God. The worst part is that we often try with our limited minds to restrict a limitless God with our personal demands. Our prayers are full of timelines and rarely do we go to the alter to say, "Lord let your will be done." Most people know exactly what they want and when they would prefer it to manifest in their lives. The problem is that because we view time so differently from God, we run the risk of being impatient and getting ahead of Him. Your prayers go from, "Lord, I would like to be married by the time I am 25 and have all of my children by age 30." At age 29 you're still single so the prayer changes a little. "Lord, I am 29 and I would really like to be married by at least 32 and have my first child right away." However, now you are approaching age 33, single, and absolutely no prospects of a husband or wife. This is where we allow time (which is our greatest resource) to become our greatest inhibitor.

We either become paralyzed by fear that we will never receive what we've asked of God, or we decide He is taking too long and take things into our own hands. We start to view delay as denial because we didn't get exactly what we wanted within our own timeline. We begin to demand that God operate according to time as *we* know it. Our haste and misunderstanding of how God views time causes us to form relationships that were never originally meant to be. *Eternity* is a term used to express the concept of something that has no end and/or no beginning. God has no beginning or end. He operates completely separate of the realm of time. Knowing this will help you to understand why certain things happen quickly and why other things will inevitably take time.

BEFORE YOU ALLOW THE PASSING OF TIME TO FRUSTRATE YOU, REMEMBER THAT GOD IS ETERNAL.

Throughout the Bible we can see examples of how God used time to grow and groom His children. Similar to the old Polaroid pictures, the development of many characters in the Bible came over time. Each of these important Biblical stories illustrated a significant difference in God's perspective of time versus our own. Depending on what we want from God, lapses of time are often viewed as unfavorable in our lives. However, many of the stories throughout the Bible show just how unmoved God is by the concept of time. Everything has happened in its rightful time and season since the beginning of creation.

In the story of Abraham's wife Sarah (originally Sarai), we see God use time to build a level of faith inside her that would be unprecedented. The book of Genesis reveals that Sarah wanted to have a child with Abraham but was unable to conceive. For many years she carried this burden and prayed for a child. It is important to remember that Sarah lived in a time when a woman's worth was measured by her ability to bare children. Barrenness must have made Sarah (although wealthy and beautiful) feel insignificant. Finally, when both Sarah and Abraham were old in age, God reveals to Abraham that he would have a son. Sarah overhears this news and laughs because she and her husband were both so advanced in age, she could never fathom having a child. Sure enough, God's promise is fulfilled and Sarah becomes a first-time mother well into her 90s. She named her son Isaac, which means "laughter". While Sarah laughed at God and the idea of becoming a mother so late in life,

God probably laughed at her inability to recognize just how powerful He was! The lesson here was that God is not on "man's" timetable. Miracles happen each and every day. Only when we take our minds off of the true power and omnipotence of God do we begin to see the limitations of our own human condition.

In the story of Joseph, we see him betrayed by his own brothers due to jealousy. Joseph had the ability to interpret dreams and as a result was called "the dreamer" by his siblings. Joseph was falsely accused and thrown into jail for a crime he did not commit. He remained confined for two years. Joseph was imprisoned at what most would consider the prime of his life. Joseph was a slave turned prisoner, but God used that time of imprisonment to prepare him for a purpose much greater. The Pharaoh of Egypt knew Joseph had the ability to interpret dreams and decided to use his skills as an advantage. Joseph's skills proved to be so highly beneficial, he was released from prison and appointed to ruler of Egypt.

Can you imagine how Joseph felt as the days, months, and years rolled by after being falsely accused and imprisoned? What trials have you had to just sit still and trust God to get you through? Did it last much longer than you'd expected? It is important to look at how God ever so brilliantly used time as a resource to groom Joseph for his future. Patience, resourcefulness, and wisdom were just a few of Joseph's character traits that were acquired from imprisonment. Joseph not only rose from slavery to leadership, but he was made significantly effective in that position by the season of tribulation he had to endure. Sometimes we have to be put in dire situations over an extended length of time in order to truly yield change from within. No one ever said life would be trouble free. God's only promise was that He would never put more on you than you could withstand.

The Biblical references of time and how it was often used as an invaluable catalyst for personal growth are endless! Joshua suffered in the wilderness for 40 years. John the Baptist spent much of his life preparing for his ministry only for his life to end soon after it began. The story of Jesus Christ was very similar as His ministry began at age 30 and he was crucified at the age of 33. The Apostle Paul spent a lot of time in prison, however singlehandedly made the most contributions to the New Testament and the advancement of the gospel of Christ.

IT'S NOT HOW MUCH TIME YOU HAVE, RATHER WHAT YOU DOING WITH YOUR TIME.

Now before you start to beat yourself up about your current age or where you are in life versus where you feel you should be, stop and think for a minute. As long as you have breath in your lungs, you have not yet accomplished all God has required of you in this life. You are still alive because someone needs you. What are you doing with the time you are being given? What are you doing with the hours, minutes, and seconds of each day that you've been granted? Life is a gift and we are all on (as many would say) borrowed time. Before we were created, our days on this earth were numbered by the Creator. You must endeavor to live a life that illustrates both your full understanding and respect for time and its finiteness in the physical realm.

Have you ever stopped to really consider the difference between being alive and living? Are you a part of that ever growing sub group classified as the "living dead"? Those are the people who wake up, shower, get dressed, drive to "jobs" of which they are uninterested, work, drive home, eat, watch TV, go to sleep, and get up by the grace of God to do it all over again. These are the people considered to be "living" by definition solely because they have a pulse and are breathing. However, these people are far from alive. The living dead wander aimlessly throughout life without passion or purpose. It is important to note that many of these people *did* have dreams, goals, aspirations and desires at one point. However, the roller coaster of life and its sometimes frightening experiences, have managed to both mentally and physically paralyze them. These types of people would rather convince themselves they no longer want certain things than to feel the sting of not having them after being knocked down by circumstances beyond their control. The determination required to get back up and try one more time is often nowhere to be found. The passion and purpose that once burned within have been replaced by fear and anxiety. Unfortunately, the "living dead" get to a point where they have conditioned themselves to avoid feeling disappointment anymore.

Are you one of those people who have lofty ideas, but find implementation to be your biggest issue? Are you part of the living dead? God can afford to move at a pace that is not affected by time. We cannot. Life is a gift that many of us fail to appreciate. We often function under the assumption that time is some obscure concept and we have more of it than we can stand. The truth is, there is someone your age who is no longer here or currently fighting for their life. When you consider the reality of how relatively short life is, then you will see that time is a gift and should be treated as such. Those of us who have the privilege of life do not have the right to squander time that someone else would have given everything for, if possible. Think about what time means to you. Think about the life you are currently living and how your actions or inaction serve as a reflection of your true value of time. Don't despise the passing of time. We are living in a time where everything is instantaneous and there is no genuine appreciation for development. We often seek profound, favorable results but don't want to go through the entire process. Yet similar to the metamorphosis of a butterfly, change that happens over time can yield something quite beautiful!

EVERYTHING AND ANYTHING THAT IS OF AUTHENTIC VALUE TOOK TIME FOR CREATION.

Diamonds take millions of years to form under the earth. A 3mm pearl will take about five years to form inside of an oyster. You must get to a point where you understand the passing of time can be beneficial. Absence of work and effort during the passing of time is wasteful. On the contrary, the passing of time with proactivity and purposeful action can never be considered a waste.

Many of us are waiting on God passively, watching time go by, and getting frustrated with the absence of what we feel should have happened already. Waiting on God should not be something you ever do passively. Your wait on God should be full of expectation that nurtures a life full of action. As a faithful Christian, there has to be certainty that what you've asked God for is already in progress. You can't be sure when your blessing will manifest, but you know for sure it is on the way. If in fact you are a faithful servant of God knowing what you desire is on its way, why wait passively? Why not ensure your words and actions align with what it is that you are expecting God to do?

If it has been your dream to purchase your first home, begin to build your savings account and practice fiscal responsibility now. Make sure you are gathering all of the resources necessary so that when the blessing comes you will be able to capitalize on the opportunity. Don't wait for the blessing to get here in order to begin preparation. Learn how to *stay* ready so you never have to *get* ready. Time is not the enemy as long as you are using it wisely and can remain in a paradigm of expectation.

We've already established that everyone gets 24 hours in a day. However, the real mystery is figuring out what separates one individual from the other in terms of success and goal attainment. Every day we are overwhelmed with opportunities that we must either accept or reject as related to time. Situations can range from something as simple as a ringing telephone to an impromptu trip to the shopping mall. In order to be successful in achieving our goals it is highly important that we learn how to prioritize. You need to know when it is time to work and when it is appropriate to allow some interruption to your work flow. It is your responsibility to find a work/life balance and remain intentional about how you spend your time.

In actuality, time management *should* be more feasible now than it ever was. With time and labor saving technology we have at our fingertips like washing machines, cellular phones, computers, and cars, we technically now have more available time than ever. Yet the irony here is that although advances in modern technology have saved us time, we are not using that time constructively. If you have a dishwasher and no longer wash dishes manually, what are you doing with the forty-five minutes to an hour that you've gained? The washing machine and dryer have taken the place of a far more time consuming process that used to take hours and prohibit multitasking. What are you doing with the time you have while the washing machine or dryer is spinning? For the individual that has not yet learned to manage their time, the answer is either absolutely nothing or something of very little significance and therein lies the problem.

While these inventions should have given us more time to be productive, the over usage of technology has actually proven to have an adverse effect on our culture. Due to the latest technologies we are currently dealing with a consistent collision between our personal and business lives. There was once a time when one could leave the office and it was acceptable to be inaccessible until the following business day. Today while we can physically leave the office, access to cellular phones and the Internet help to facilitate ongoing business communication well past office hours. Now more than ever, there is a need to define your own work/life boundaries and prioritize in order to stay on track with goal attainment. Without definitive boundaries, you run the risk of failing to accomplish goals that you've set in work or your personal life.

The ongoing presence of television and persuasion of marketing can also cause us to be susceptible to a variety of distractions. The prevalence of advertising and the extensiveness of today's marketing strategies leave us all open to being distracted at almost any time of the day. The major problem here is that often while we should be concentrating on a certain project or important task, we are being bombarded with sights and sounds that are designed to promote a completely different agenda. Having the ability to manage time is highly important to all who are proactively seeking goal attainment.

DECIDE TODAY WHAT IS MOST IMPORTANT TO YOU AND WORTH YOUR TIME.

Different areas of our lives will always require our time in some form or another. We are pulled in multiple directions on a daily basis. Depending on where you are at in your life right now, your roles can range from parent to executive and everything in between. Time management is important because it is the most important tool in the box to help build a successful life. The truth is, if you are unable give definition to every aspect of your life and the time you spend doing it, you will continue to allow for the misappropriation of your most valuable resource.

Unless we can learn to truly appreciate why time management is so significant, there is always the risk of delaying our own personal growth and progression in life. We cannot control how much time we are given in the earthly realm. However, we are able to control what we do with the time we are gifted. Take into consideration that time is something that cannot be saved, bought, exchanged, or even borrowed past God's will for your life. Once you genuinely start to view time as the invaluable commodity it is, you will notice a change in your everyday habits. Your lifestyle will change completely. How you use your time today will yield the results of tomorrow and shape your reality. If we are only given one life to live here on earth, it is imperative we use the time we have to live our best lives!

Successful time management involves incorporation of the following:

#1: <u>Planning</u>: Effective time management will require you to learn plan effectively. In order to become a "pro" at planning, you will need practice! For at least a month, make the commitment to retrain yourself in this area. Get into a great habit of planning your day well in advance. Each day, take the time out to prepare a "to do" list. Write down all of the important activities that need to be done that day as well as the time you are allotting yourself for the completion of each activity. The list should be in order; activities with the highest priority coming before those that do not demand your immediate attention. Complete each task one by one and refrain from beginning new tasks before the previous task on the list has been completed. Of course there will be days when even the most detailed list and best of intentions will not matter. Life happens and everything cannot be planned to a tee!

#2: <u>Goal Setting and Objectives</u>: When we work aimlessly without goals or objectives in life it is similar to setting sail on the ocean without a compass to provide direction. It doesn't matter the size, but there should always be definitive goals that you are actively pursuing. From weight loss to entrepreneurship, it is your responsibility to identify those things you genuinely want for yourself and get about the business of attaining them one at a time. Dare to dream again and learn to set targets for yourself. Make sure to start out by setting goals that are achievable within realistic timeframes. Goal setting on a grand scale at first may prove to be discouraging if you have not set realistic expectations. As you begin to attain goals in different areas of your life you will feel amazingly accomplished and full of self-confidence. Once you get to a place where goal setting is the norm, challenge yourself to take risks. Not every goal has to be lofty, but every now and again, set a goal that is far beyond your wildest imagination!

#3: <u>Deadlines</u>: Have you ever noticed how well you can stick to a deadline when it comes to your job? However, if it is a personal goal that you've set for yourself, somehow procrastination sets in and deadlines are long forgotten. When you make promises to yourself, learn how to keep them. If there is a goal you would like to accomplish by the end of the year, then it is imperative you do all necessary to accomplish it. Why are we so motivated to adhere to deadlines when imposed by others, but we lack the self-discipline to follow our own? Set deadlines for yourself and work diligently to complete each task *ahead* of the deadlines. Learn how to self-govern and be result driven without extrinsic motivation. Once you learn how to produce within the deadlines you have set for yourself, you will be well on your way.

#4: <u>Delegating</u>: Someone once said, "If you want something right, you have to do it yourself." In many ways, that statement is quite truthful. However, those who are excellent stewards of their time have successfully learned to delegate. Simply put, there comes a time when you must solicit the expertise of other people to get a particular job done. You cannot do it all on your own. Behind the most powerful, influential people on the face of the earth you will find a team of individuals who make significant contributions to their overall success. Learning to delegate will allow for the task to be done in a timely manner, but also by someone who may (quite frankly) be better suited for that task than you. Learning to delegate will also free up time to tackle other tasks that may be more time sensitive. There is not always enough time in a day to take care of the lesser prioritized tasks. That is where your ability to delegate will prove to be highly beneficial.

#5: <u>Prioritizing</u>: Learning to prioritize is extremely critical when building time management skills. Everything can't be classified as a priority. If *every*thing is a priority, then nothing is really a priority. Get comfortable with the idea of identifying and listing tasks by importance or urgency. Knowing what can wait and what must be done right away will always yield optimal results. At first look, many of the tasks we are responsible for accomplishing throughout the day seem equally important. However, if you look a little closer, you will be able to identify many of the activities labeled "urgent" are not really important in the grand scheme. Timing is everything! Develop the habit of doing the right thing at the right time. Work done at the wrong time can have an adverse effect on your personal life. Vice versa, any social interaction done at the wrong time can hinder any professional goals you have set for yourself.

As you become a better steward of your time, you will notice a change in every area of your life. Most importantly, you will become more aware of the long list of potential time wasters. A "time waster" is activity you engage in that has little to no value and distracts you from reaching your goals. Time wasters are all around and were designed to keep you off track. They come in all different forms -- some quite obvious while others are obscure and not readily identifiable.

Obvious

- Commercially available since the early 1920's, televisions can be found in the homes of Americans all across the country. In 2009, the results of Neilson's "Three Screen Report" concluded the average American watches approximately 153 hours of TV per month at home, and that is a 1.2% increase from 2008. That was over 5 years ago and times have changed! Television is indeed a form of entertainment and there is nothing wrong with enjoying that luxury. However, it is essential for you to begin to sharpen your awareness of how much of your time is being spent in front of the television. Often times when we fail to accomplish a particular goal within a set time, the first thing we say is "If I only had more time." The truth is that we are all given the same 24 hours in a day. The most successful people in the world do not take time for granted and are highly unlikely to spend 4 hours of their day watching television. Time is your most valuable resource and it must be spent wisely.

- We live in the age of the Internet and many of us utilize this form of technology every single day. Whether at home or work, there is always the opportunity to waste valuable time browsing various websites. What started off as a log on to simply pay your cellular phone bill turned into a 2-hour Internet shopping session on your favorite store's website! It happened so fast that you don't even know where the time went. More than likely you will shrug it off and promise to be more diligent "tomorrow". The problem here is that the same distractions that exist today will also exist tomorrow. The distractions will always be there. The change will have to come from within you! You will have to decide that whatever goal you have set for yourself is too important to waste any time engaging in activities that in no way advance your personal goal agenda.

- Telephones aren't what they used to be. Today, the cellular phone is literally a hand held computer, calculator, navigational system, game console and more! If the phone is not being used for interpersonal communication, there are a variety of other options. Without a keen awareness and respect for time, it is possible to spend a significant amount of time each day playing games or engaging in social media using the phone. Social media has become extremely prevalent in today's society. It seems like everyone is tuned in to Facebook, Twitter, Instagram, or MySpace. While these avenues are a great way to stay connected, if you are not careful these forms of social media can also rob you of precious time you cannot get back.

The television, computer, and cell phone can all be considered fairly obvious time wasters. However, there are things that we continuously engage in each day that are less obvious, but just as effective in wasting valuable time. It is important that you educate yourself on what these things are and help to build your own awareness.

Obscure

- **Gossip**: Mark Twain once said, "He gossips habitually; he the common wisdom to keep still that deadly enemy of man, his own tongue." We've all at one point or another engaged in lengthy "gossip sessions" about other people and what is going on in their lives. Plainly put, all the time spent gossiping is time not being used to attain your own goals. Do your very best to steer clear of conversations that involve gossiping and otherwise empty rhetoric. If you are going to spend time talking, let it be edifying conversation that benefits all parties involved.

- **Shopping**: Well intentioned, you've gone into one of your favorite stores for a few necessary household items. Before you know it, there is a shopping cart full of items and you have spent almost two hours in the store. In a situation like this, you've managed to waste both time *and* money. As your time management skill sets continue to develop, you will be able to better assess each scenario as it comes. You will have the strength to self-discipline and remind yourself that there were only 30 minutes allotted for this trip to the store. Any activity extending that time frame will automatically be characterized as a "time waster".

- **Social Events**: All work and no play are unacceptable. Making a conscious effort to ensure work/life balance is extremely important. However, be careful that you do not allow your social life to adversely impact your ability to manage time effectively. How many times have you gone to a social event for the sake of having "something to do"? We've all been there before and there is nothing wrong with making sure new life experiences don't pass you by! But before you get all dressed up and head out to attend an event that is truly of little importance to you, ask yourself what you could or should be doing instead. If weight loss is a goal of yours, perhaps a trip to the gym would be more beneficial and dual purposed. You will work out your body while being in a position to meet new people!

- **"Helping"**: Being helpful, empathetic and caring for others whether it be friends, family, and/or strangers is wonderful. However, being an excellent steward of your time will significantly decrease the probability of allowing other people and their life crises to waste any of your time. Before you spend any significant amount of time consistently tapping into your inner "counselor", consider the fact that your time is valuable. Don't allow your kindness or helpfulness to work against you. Refrain from acquiring the "people pleaser" role. People pleasers typically have difficulty understanding their behaviors are often a waste of their own valuable time. This type of person is far more concerned with doing things to please other people. More often than not, they suffer as a result of wasted time.

Becoming an effective governor of your time is essential to the overall success of your restoration process. In order to have something you've never had, you'll have to do something you've never done. The 24-hour span in a day is still the same. Your life will begin to change the minute you've truly learned to take back control of your time. Discipline yourself and get into the habit of engaging in a lifestyle that will contribute to a work life balance. It is highly important for you to have a social life and be open to beautiful new experiences. However, it is equally important to use time as the invaluable resource that it is to both establish and accomplish your own goals.

Prayer:

Lord, as I read and understand your Word, I notice how you have often used time as a holding chamber for personal growth. Help me to recognize the time you have given me on earth is valuable and not to be squandered. Sometimes I get impatient and allow the passing of time to make me anxious about things I cannot control. Help me to always trust in your timing and remember that waiting on you does not mean it is ok to remain in a state of passivity. While I wait on you I should be proactively preparing myself for the blessings that I have prayed for! Thank you Lord for life and the gift of time! May I always remember how fragile life is, and how fleeting time can be. Amen!

CHAPTER 10: REFLECTIONS

Chapter 10 was designed to help you begin to view the concept of time differently. Answer the questions below to help facilitate more thought about time and its importance during your restoration.

1. Time is the great equalizer as we are all given the same amount each day. How well do you currently manage your time?

   _____

   _____

   _____

   _____

2. The key to managing your time effectively is being able to identify your current patterns. List some of the things you are currently doing that can be categorized as "time wasters"

   _____

   _____

   _____

   _____

3. After reading Chapter 10, what is your new understanding of how God views time? How does that help you while waiting for God to move in your life?

_____

_____

_____

_____

CHAPTER 11: WE ALL GO THROUGH IT

You weren't the first person to experience a failed relationship or rejection. And you will not be the last. What you are experiencing right now is something that we have all gone through at some point in our lives. That is not to in any way minimize the pain you feel, but rather to establish what you are going through is normal and this too shall pass. The most important thing to remember is that while this experience will soon be in your rearview mirror, it is up to you to learn everything you possibly can while going through it. If not, you will find yourself back in a similar situation sooner than later.

Whether you know it or not, you've been programmed regarding relationships. Prior to your restoration process, your relationships have mirrored what you've seen. Regardless of gender, race, age, or socio-economic status we are all preconditioned as far as relationships go. Our parents, grandparents, aunts, uncles and other relatives have given us a mental blueprint of what our relationships should look like. The relationship dynamics you've seen in those closest to you are the ones you have subconsciously accepted as the norm. There are young girls who have grown into financially and emotionally needy women because those were the behaviors to which they were exposed by the women closest to them. The truth is that with God's grace we can become any and everything we desire. You don't *have* to make the same mistakes as others. However, we do have a tendency to emulate that which we see. If growing up as a young girl you distinctly remember your mother's excessive dependency on a man, then it is highly likely you will feel most comfortable in a relationship of that nature. That young girl has now turned into a woman convinced excessive dependency is the norm in her relationships. If growing up as a young boy you remember most a father with inept communication skill sets, but strong ability to financially provide for the family, it is highly likely that is what your relationship may look like. That young boy has now turned into a man who is predisposed to believing that providing for his family is the extent of his relationship obligations; it doesn't matter that there are major communication issues.

YOU CAN HAVE THE RELATIONSHIP YOU HAVE ALWAYS DREAMED.

Decide today that your future relationship will break the generational curse of dysfunction you may have seen all of your life. It doesn't matter what the relationships you've seen were like. What matters is your definition of a healthy relationship and what you desire for yourself. Now that you have gone through your season of self, you are in a much better position to say what you want or don't want in your life. Prior to really getting to know yourself, your relationships mirrored that of what you considered normal. You now know that what someone else deems normal may not necessarily align favorably with your personal definition. A healthy relationship to someone who is financially dependent would be as simple as having a mate who can fulfill that specific need. A healthy relationship for someone who is emotionally dependent would be solely based on their partner's ability to cater to that need. Your definition of healthy and successful relationship may be multi-faceted with considerably higher expectations of your partner. Or, your definition may be simplistic and require nothing more than open communication, honesty, and respect; money is of no concern. It all depends on who you are and what you want in your life.

You have the power to manifest the relationships that you want for yourself. People will only treat you the way you continuously allow. If respect and honesty are non-negotiable within your relationship, then those are standards you must set and refuse to waver on at any time. Even still, if the relationship is a Godsend, it will not come a minute before He feels you are genuinely ready. Timing is everything in life. God will not send you the relationship He desires for you to have until you are completely ready. That being said, you must be patient and recognize there will be waiting involved. Anything that starts too quickly and in poor timing will end the same way.

The waiting game will require unprecedented levels of faith. If you are not careful, you will be overcome with impatience. You will be anxious to date and be in a relationship because that is what you see around you. It is highly likely you will become angry with God and begin to question the process. After you question the process, you will come face to face with temptation to just do what you want to do because "this is taking too long". However, we've already established in Chapter 12 that God often uses time as a chamber for personal growth. Instead of whining and crying about when the love of your life is going to show up, seek God for counsel. Find out what you are supposed to be doing and learning before he/she shows up in your life.

When you are experiencing a season of singleness (especially if being single is not something you are used to) it can be overwhelming. It will feel like just about everyone you've ever known is in a relationship and you are the only one experiencing being single. Everyone around you seems to be so incredibly happy! Part of you is happy for them and the other part of you is saddled with fear, anxiety, and yes jealousy! It may even be your very best friend and part of you can't help but to want it to be your turn. These are natural reactions to what you are experiencing and you should not beat yourself up about how you feel. Be honest with yourself about your emotional state. It is okay to acknowledge your feelings but it is not okay to immerse yourself in them -- especially if they are emotions that are not beneficial to you.

Patience is the key ingredient to the success of any relationships on the horizon for you. When we get ahead of God things will inevitably turn to ruin. More than likely that last sentence read like a real bold generalization. However if you look back over your life, you will find it to be true. Each of the relationships you have been involved in to date have for some reason or another ended. If you are honest with yourself you will be able to admit that these were relationships you entered without waiting on God for directive. We make mistakes and will continue to do so as it is in our human nature. God is not man and therefore does not make mistakes. Any serious relationships that did not last were because you lacked the ability to *wait*.

Waiting for the right person doesn't need to be a state of passivity. You should be actively waiting with expectation. While you are waiting for the relationship you desire, there should be action going on! Keep yourself busy. Now that you have learned to enjoy your own company, the world is your oyster! Nurture your interests and begin to try new activities. Try a painting class and explore the possibility of unleashing your inner Picasso. Sign up for a cooking class and learn how to make healthy, gourmet meals for yourself and possibly your future spouse. Go experience the limited time exhibit being offered at the museum; you never know who you will run into while there. You have been wanting to learn how to Salsa dance for years now, so go sign up for a class! Weight loss is a goal you've put off for too long. Join the gym and get started today on attaining the goals you've set for a new healthy lifestyle. Take some time out and volunteer at the neighborhood soup kitchen; there is a beautiful soul there that could use your smile. While you are waiting for God to bless you with the relationship of your dreams, you must *keep moving*!

Waiting for your relationship while in an active state let's God know you are ready. And while you are waiting for Mr. or Mrs. Right it is equally important for you to use this time to check your motives.

Ask yourself all of the difficult questions necessary to get the answers you need:

1. **Do you *really* believe you are ready to be in a relationship?** Only you and your Creator know the true answer to that question. Set aside age, gender, socio-economic statuses, societal norms and all other potentially influential reasoning for wanting to be in a relationship right now and ask yourself: Are you genuinely ready for a relationship or have you been influenced by outside sources? Have you allowed society to dictate what should be next for you? Have you reached a certain age and are now feeling anxious about not being in a relationship at this time in your life? Are you afraid that if you do not do it now, your chance for love will never come?

2. **Are you simply tired of being alone?** Some of us want to be in a relationship right now and are not willing to wait a minute longer for multiple reasons. Some have been single for so long that we feel as though we are being robbed of an amazing experience and time is passing us by! Others have not spent any significant amount of time as a single person and being single feels very unnatural. Fortunately for you, the "Season of Self" was to help you modify your way of thinking about being single. You should now know with utmost certainty that being single can be amazingly beautiful. More importantly, being single for a significant amount of time will allow you to get to know yourself in ways that being fully submerged in a partnership will not. If you are seeking to be in a relationship for the sole reason of not wanting to be alone any longer, you must reconsider.

Be careful! It is here that people typically start to attempt to rush their restoration process and some abandon it altogether. When we have our hearts and minds set on something, it is difficult to wait on it with no definitive information on when it's coming. Waiting on God without having a definitive time in which things will be back on course can be extremely frustrating! However in Isaiah 40:31 reads, "Yet those who wait for the Lord will gain new strength; They will mount up with wings like eagles, they will run and not get tired, they will walk and not become weary."

Do not attempt to get back into a relationship until you are certain it is time to do so. While you are going through your period of waiting, do not allow anything or anyone to distract you. Anything in the process of being restored is considered to be off limits until completed. That is the same for you. Getting involved too soon and with the wrong person again can have severe consequences.

THERE WILL BE ATTEMPTS TO GET YOU OFF TARGET, BUT REMAIN STEADFAST.

We live in the age of social media. Personal information is shared and up for public scrutiny each and every day. Someone is getting married this upcoming Saturday. Someone just announced a baby boy is on the way. Someone just got engaged to their high school sweetheart. Don't be surprised if while you are working out the details of your life, it seems like everything around you is changing and you are standing still. Be mindful about the influence of social media on your emotional state. Do not torture yourself by spending any significant amount of time comparing yourself to others. What is for you is for you. When the time is right, your relationship will come. In the interim, you have no business comparing yourself or your journey to that of other people. By doing so, you are in essence telling God what is best for you and when. Rest well knowing that you serve a God who knew you before you were in physical existence and knows exactly what you need and when to give it to you. Avoid the pitfalls of impatience and anxiousness. There is no pity party like the one you can throw when you feel like things aren't moving fast enough for you.

Avoid the trap of social media like Facebook that gives many people the opportunity to shape and create their own realities through pictures and posts. People tend to paint the picture they would prefer you see of their lives. Wedding photos, vacation photos, new baby photos, engagement rings, and date nights just to name a few. All of those things are incredibly heart-warming and beautiful. However, the reality is that no one hired a photographer to snap pictures of infidelity or videotape the huge argument the "perfect couple" may have had the week prior. It is important that you genuinely understand what you see is not always the reality of a given situation.

You don't know if the beautiful pictures and posts you see on social media are one hundred percent authentic. You don't know the financial status of that couple. You don't know the details of their relationship. The post read, "Flowers sent to me by my love" followed by a picture of the most beautiful bouquet you've ever seen. However, you have no idea what prompted the floral gifting. Perhaps the flowers were simply a gift to say, "I love you". Perhaps the flowers were an "I'm sorry for hurting you or I apologize for my mistake." Whatever the case may be, you need to understand that words and pictures can be and (on social media) are often used to put out a limited message.

You can't run your race as efficiently as possible if you are busy paying attention to other people. If you look closely at the form of each of the track and field champions around the world, you will notice something very important. When they are on that track they refrain from looking to the left or right of them. The most important goal is to stay in their specific lane and get to the finish line first. All of the champions look straight ahead! It is the same formula for your relationship success. Do not focus on what is going on in the lives of other people. Your restoration process is all about *you*. For this one time in your life, you have permission to be completely self-concerned. Pay little to no attention to what is going on around you in terms of other people's relationships. What people do in their relationships in no way affects you or your future relationships.

Don't whine or cry about how this person got engaged before you or how that person and their significant other are welcoming their second child. You don't know their life stories. You have no idea the sacrifices that were made to yield these blessings. You don't know the intricate details of their personal lives and most importantly you don't have the right to assume. Jealousy and envy are incredibly consuming emotions that don't hurt anyone but you. While you are sulking and complaining about what you want but don't have, you are missing out on the opportunity to enjoy what you do have! Gratitude is proof that you both recognize and appreciate all of the amazing blessings that you already have been given. Without exhibiting gratitude for blessings past and present, you may unknowingly hinder future blessings. Make it a point to focus on all of the things that you already have in your life whether big or small. Tell God you are grateful for all of the blessings you've been showered with throughout your life. Learn to be genuinely happy for others even if it seems like they are being blessed with all of the things you've ever wanted. It is not your place to decide what others deserve. God will bless you just the same when the time is right!

Many of us will ask ourselves, "What do they have that I don't?" The truth is that you don't know any details about their personal relationships with God. You don't know the sacrifices they made to obtain the desires of their hearts. The question shouldn't be: 'why is everyone seemingly in a great relationship except me?' The real question is 'am I really ready to receive the relationship that I genuinely want-- and if not-- what am I doing to get ready?' There would be nothing worse than spending your time so focused on other people that you fail to take full advantage of your restoration process.

Being single is **not** a curse and you should not treat it as such. The sad part is that many people are so focused on finding a significant other that they are missing a great opportunity for personal growth. There is a level of self-awareness that can only be reached when you have spent significant time alone getting to know yourself. Solitude is a gift and if honest, many married couples would admit sometimes they just want to be left alone to their own thoughts. Whether it's an impromptu vacation, a day at the spa, or a sporting event with awesome tickets because you wanted to splurge, being single has its benefits. Embrace your singleness and use this time to your full advantage.

Below are the results of an interview with a Christian single that has experienced devastating heartbreak. Heartbreak is something we've all experienced at one point and time in our lives. The purpose of sharing the responses of the interview was simply to illustrate that while each broken relationship is different, there are many experiences we have and emotions we feel in the aftermath that illustrate a beautiful commonality. There is power in testimony and hearing about how God's extended grace has lifted many from emotionally consuming situations.

Interviewee: Female, mid-thirties, corporate executive, single, no children

Question 1: Were you able to forgive the person who hurt you? Did it take a long time? If so, how has forgiving the person who hurt you changed your life?

Answer: When the relationship first ended, there was not an ounce of forgiveness in my heart. I felt used, abused, lied to, and completely disrespected. I was hurting and I wanted him to hurt as well. As time went on, the pain and anger I felt began to physically take a toll on me. I was experiencing panic attacks, changes in sleeping patterns, disinterest in things that had once excited me, and just an overwhelming physical heaviness. It took a very long time for me to even consider forgiving the person who broke my heart, but it got to a point where I genuinely understood I would have to do it in order to move forward. The anger I had toward that individual was starting to consume *me*! Forgiving him has literally lifted a weight off of my shoulders. I have not forgotten what transpired, nor do I feel like any of it was ok, but I did choose to forgive to help myself get on with my life. I knew there was something better out there for me and it would never come if I was not open to receiving it. When you are so angry and bitter, it's impossible to draw anything positive into to your life. Forgiving has helped me to realize that I am a lot stronger than I ever gave myself credit for.

Question 2: How long have you been single?

Answer: I have been single for almost 3 years now. It feels like forever! (Laughs)

Question 3: What are some of the benefits of living a single life?

Answer: The first thing that comes to mind is that I am solely responsible for myself. The needs of a husband or children are not yet a responsibility of mine just yet. Decisions that I make from day to day are coming from me and as long as I consider it beneficial, I am free to do it. In a relationship it would be different and certain decisions would be made *after* consulting with my significant other. Right now it is nice to just be able to pick up and go, make purchases based on my wants, and splurge every now and then.

Question 4: What are some of the not-so-great aspects of living a single life?

Answer: Loneliness. Sometimes I come home from a long day at work and sit on my couch only to realize there is no one there but me at home. I would like to experience the joys of coming home to a husband who asks me how my day was. I would love to experience children who run to meet me at the door with hugs and kisses. The silence in my home can be so loud at times. It's hard to explain. Then of course there are those dreaded invites to social events and sometimes I strongly consider not going because I don't have a "plus one". Over time I have learned to enjoy movies and dinner by myself but I would honestly love to have a partner to share these experiences with, you know?

Question 5: As a Christian, what are some of the challenges you've experienced being single? Are you currently abstaining? If not, what is your reasoning? If so, do you find that difficult to do in a society that promotes casual sex? Do you ever explore the topic of sex with someone you are dating? If so, how is it approached?

Answer: Wow! That is a loaded question and very interesting. I can confirm that it is extremely challenging dating these days and it goes far beyond the fact that I am a Christian. I am currently abstaining and while I would love to say it is only because of my strong Christian values, if I am honest, there is more to it than that. Through the years I have come to understand that sex is truly powerful. What I decided to do was avoid giving the best I have to offer to people who were unworthy. Doing so only made me feel inferior and unworthy of the type of love my heart genuinely desires. I think we all want to know that we are physically attractive to someone else. However, it got to the point where flattery was no longer impressive. I wanted much more from my past relationship partners than they were willing to give. I grew tired of feeling like I was being used and thrown away. Sex is an extremely personal decision and I just genuinely believe a pre-requisite should be commitment. I don't engage in casual sex any longer. Whether it be the possibility of endangering my physical health, emotional setbacks, or additional financial obligations due to an unplanned pregnancy, there is nothing casual about any of the ramifications of sex. Therefore, I choose to treat having sex as the powerful and potentially life altering act that it is. In addition, as I've gotten older my tastes have changed. Empty, emotionally disconnected sex used to serve its purpose for physical gratification. As I have evolved, so have my needs and expectations. To answer you with full candor, I do find it increasingly difficult to navigate through dating in a society that promotes casual sex. However, it isn't because I waver on my conviction. It is more so the challenge to get and keep the attention of men who (Christian or not) are not abstaining, genuinely do not wish to do so, and are openly expressing their disappointment with my decision. I make sure to discuss the expectations of sex early on. I don't really see the point in continuing to date someone who has a different viewpoint on a topic so incredibly important.

Question 6: **Are you currently dating? If so, how long did it take for you to start dating again after the breakup?**

Answer: Right now I am not dating but I am open to it. To be honest with you, I started to date shortly after the breakup and not surprisingly I was attracting all of the wrong type of attention. I think in retrospect, it was because I was so hurt that I was simply looking for acceptance and attention from whomever was giving it at the time. One failed relationship attempt after the other, I finally decided to just chill out and focus on myself. Chasing after something that feels ever eluding is just so exhausting. At some point I came to realize that there *had* to be a reason why Mr. Right hadn't found me yet. Instead of focusing on everyone else, I knew I had to look within. So that's where I'm at right now. I'm working on *me*.

Question 7: **What is your definition of being equally yoked? Is that a requirement for your next relationship? Why or why not?**

Answer: For the longest time I thought equally yoked meant I would need to date someone who made the same amount of money as me; someone who was my equal financially. What I realize now is that equally yoked has nothing to do with what the man makes and everything to do with what makes up the man. It's about who he is as a person, goals, and life philosophies. We don't need to be interested in the same sports or love the same types of music. I think it would be great to have certain things in common with your mate. But being equally yoked is about having a similar mindset. Do we share the same views on what is moral or immoral; ethical or unethical? It is important to establish goals and aspirations to see if our lives are going in two completely different directions. Being equally yoked is most important in my next relationship. I personally believe that is one of the most important components to the relationship lasting. A relationship is like building a house and I think being equally yoked helps to build a very strong foundation for that house. For me it is really not optional.

Question 8: How do you counteract the fear or anxiety that may set in about wanting a relationship and not having it manifested after what you feel is a significant amount of time?

Answer: Well I used to counteract that fear by serial dating. If I am consistently dating and keeping myself busy, then I don't have time to focus on what I don't have. Today, I remind myself to take it day by day. It gets difficult at times; I cannot lie about that at all. I am not old, but I am no longer in my 20s and I would love to be a mother one day. As a woman you get to a certain age and you do feel pressure to get things moving so that you can have a child before health risks increase for you and the baby. However, as a Christian I have also learned to just rest in my faith. I am a woman who enjoys being in control of her life and making things happen. I've been blessed with an amazing career but it is impossible to get to such a level in a male dominated industry and not be action oriented. So learning to sit still and wait for the right timing proved to be difficult for me at first. It just felt more natural to go get what I wanted versus waiting for it to come to me. But as I leaned into my faith I have come to understand that this is something that should never be rushed. God knows what I want and need. I just need to be ready when it comes."

Question 9: Are you genuinely happy for family, friends, and associates alike on social media who all seem to be in happy relationships? Do you ever feel jealous? If so, please explain.

Answer: I would be a liar if I told you I didn't grapple with jealousy for a very long time. It seems like almost every last one of my friends from high school has gotten married and had children within the past three to four years. I have definitely sat in my bed with the pint of ice cream crying out to God "Why me?" and "When is my turn?!" It took me a very long time to genuinely be happy for my friends. Don't get me wrong. I love them all dearly, but I'm human and while I was happy for them, I also felt slighted. Almost like God was blessing everyone except me. I didn't understand why giving me a husband and children (what I want most) was so difficult for him to do! But one day I had an "Aha" moment. I was at an awesome winter retreat and had the opportunity to spend time with other amazing Christian women. One of them said, "God giving you the man of your dreams is EASY. It takes no effort for Him to do that at all…" I thought to myself that if it takes God no effort at all to bring me a husband, where *is* he?! That's when I realized the desires of my heart were being held up by *me*, not God's ability. There was a reason why I had not yet met the man of my dreams and I realized it was because *I* had work to do.

Question 10: What have you learned about yourself during your season of singleness?

Answer: I think what I've learned most is patience. And that is something that is applicable in both my personal and professional life. I will not always get what I want at the exact time that I want it.

Also, I've learned to strengthen my faith muscle. My relationship with God has grown and matured tremendously and I am grateful for where I am in life right now. I know for sure I am exactly where I am meant to be and today I am satisfied with that. There are so many beautiful and exciting things happening in my life right now that I can't bring myself to do anything but be grateful for each blessing!

Prayer: *Lord, I thank you for this experience. I know that while it may feel like I am the only one on earth who has ever felt this level of pain, I am not alone. Thank you for each and every valley of difficulty I've had to experience. I know one day I may be able to use my experiences to help someone else that is going through a similar situation. I am not the only one to experience heartbreak and there are many others out there. Today, I want to lift up each and every one who is currently battling with depression, anxiety, and or low self-esteem as a result of a failed relationship. I thank you in advance for comforting them as you have me, teaching them as you have taught me, and restoring them as you are currently restoring me. Amen!*

CHAPTER 11 *REFLECTIONS*

No one is exempt from the sting of heartbreak. It is important to always keep in mind that this is something we all go through. You are not alone. Review and answer the questions below to help reflect on Chapter 11.

1. **What does your ideal relationship look like? What are some of the most important components of a successful relationship to you? Do you believe your answer has anything to do with your exposure to certain types of relationships growing up?**

   _____

   _____

   _____

2. Do you have an issue with comparing yourself to others?
    How do you handle situations that cause envy or
    jealousy of others?

    _____

    _____

    _____

3. Are you currently everything you seek in a mate? Do you
    bring to the table all that you are requiring in a
    relationship from your partner? If not, what areas are in
    need of immediate improvement?

    _____

    _____

    _____

CHAPTER 12: EMOTIONAL INTELLIGENCE

Separate of the amazing work you are doing on the inside, nothing will impact the success of your restoration more than the relationships you engage in from here on out. Your external and internal conditions are of equal importance. In fact, if you take just a few minutes to reflect on past relationships (external) and incorporate your mindset (internal) at that particular time, you may be able to see a correlation. The types of relationships you've engaged in up until now have had everything to do with your way of thinking. If at the time you believed you were unworthy of anything good, then it only made sense to engage in relationships (personal or professional) that spoke to your perceived unworthiness.

At any given time, your relationships serve as a clear reflection of what you think of yourself. It is your responsibility to make sure that you are able to successfully manage the *right* relationships in your life. Each day you are presented with a new opportunity to build or rebuild the types of relationships that will enhance your life. Like the lyrics of the song says, "you've got to know when to hold them and when to fold them." In order to do that, you must be able to apply the tools and resources of Emotional

Intelligence. Emotional intelligence will allow you to be able to manage the emotions of yourself and others, thus setting the necessary groundwork for the building of solid, mutually beneficial relationships.

Peter Salovey and John D. Mayer (1990) defined emotional intelligence as "the ability to monitor one's own and others' feelings and emotions, to discriminate among them and to use this information to guide one's thinking and actions." Both men were in the process of trying to develop a way to measure the difference between people's abilities as related to emotions. What they found was that some people were better than others at things like solving emotion-laden issues, identifying their own emotions, and identifying the emotions of other people. After further research, Mayer and Salovey revised the definition of emotional intelligence to be "the ability to perceive emotion, integrate emotion to facilitate thought, understand emotions and to regulate emotions to promote personal growth."

EMOTIONAL INTELLIGENCE IS SIGNIFICANTLY IMPORTANT TO DEVELOP.

Your ability to understand not only your emotions, but also the emotions of others is key to successful relationship building. As you go out into the world a brand new man or woman, you must recognize the significance of the relationships you foster. Your goal attainment and overall life satisfaction will have much to do with the caliber of relationships you have. The depth and breadth of these relationships will be highly influenced by your level of emotional intelligence. Many of you have never heard of Emotional Intelligence and that is ok because it is a relatively new concept. However, it is indeed life-changing once you commit to applying its components into your everyday life. It doesn't matter that you've never heard of it before. What matters most is that after reading this chapter you will have been exposed to the concept and how powerful its implications can be in relationship constructing.

In 1995 a book written by Daniel Goleman entitled *Emotional Intelligence* was published and brought more recognition to the new concept. Three years later the same author published another book called "Working with Emotional Intelligence". Goleman revealed the skill sets that help to distinguish the star performers in the workplace from entry-level to top executive positions. An example of two recent college graduates was used to illustrate the importance of being emotionally intelligent. One of the young men was an incredibly brilliant graduate of Yale. This young man was overly confident and borderline arrogant. The other young man was not as successful academically but he was adept interpersonally. He had the ability to learn quickly and was a pleasure to work with as stated by former coworkers. Ultimately, the young man who had emotional intelligence received almost three times as many job offers upon graduation as compared to the Yale graduate. Yes, the above example specifically involved the workplace. However, emotional intelligence applies to all of the relationships you have whether business or personal. It is well worth the investment of your time to learn as much about emotional intelligence as you can.

Present day, the three main models of Emotional Intelligence are ability, mixed, and trait based. Let's first establish the differences between ability and trait based emotional intelligence. Mayer and Salovey's research helped to authenticate the ability based EI model. The model proposed that Emotional Intelligence includes four types of abilities:

- Perceiving emotions — having the ability identify to emotions in general. Whether an individual's own emotions or the emotions of others, being able to assess emotions is a significant aspect of emotional intelligence. You need to be able to empathize and understand how people are feeling at any giving point. In addition, you need to be in tuned with your *own* emotions! Often, we can become so concerned with attempting to help others emotionally, that we forget to acknowledge our own feelings.

- Using emotions — having the ability to use emotions to enhance processes such as problem solving. An individual with emotional intelligence is able to identify the emotion and use it to their positive advantage, thus creating a situation where the desired outcome is more than possible. People with "stinking thinking" may deem this a form of manipulation. However, it is very important for you to understand that using your understanding of emotions to create desirable and favorable outcomes in no way compares to manipulative behavior. As someone who has put in the hard work required throughout this restoration process, you know for certain there is limitless power in the shifting of one's paradigm.

- Understanding emotions — having the ability to comprehend emotion-laden language and to foster an appreciation for the complexity of emotions. For example, an individual who truly understands emotions has the ability to recognize that emotions are ever changing and evolving. This is incredibly important as you press forward with life and engage in new relationship building.

- Managing emotions — having the ability to regulate emotions in ourselves as well as other people. Ultimately, the emotionally intelligent individual can control their emotions whether positive or negative, and manage them to assist with goal attainment. This part of emotional intelligence is very important for those who have found it difficult in the past to either govern their own emotions or communicate with people who lack emotional control.

Further research has proposed a significant conceptual distinction between trait and ability based emotional intelligence. Trait Emotional Intelligence is an individual's *perception* of their emotional abilities. This type of emotional intelligence is about self-perceived abilities that are measured through self-report. The ability based model of emotional intelligence attempts to measure an individual's *actual* ability versus *perceived* capabilities.

Trait Emotional Intelligence Framework

Derived from earlier models, Petrides, Furnham, and Mavrovelli (2007) identified a sampling domain of trait emotional intelligence, which included 12 facets (see Figure 1.3).

(Figure 1.3) The Sampling Domain of Trait Emotional Intelligence in Adults and Adolescents

Facets	High scorers perceive themselves as...
Adaptability	...flexible and willing to adapt to new conditions.
Assertiveness	...forthright, frank, and willing to stand up for their rights.
Emotion perception (self and others)	...clear about their own and other people's feelings.
Emotion expression	...capable of communicating their feelings to others.
Emotion management (others)	...capable of influencing other people's feelings.
Emotion regulation	...capable of controlling their emotions.
Impulsiveness (low)	...reflective and less likely to give in to their urges.
Relationships	...capable of having fulfilling personal relationships.
Self-esteem	...successful and self-confident.
Self-motivation	...driven and unlikely to give up in the face of adversity.
Social awareness	...accomplished networkers with excellent

	social skills.
Stress management	...capable of withstanding pressure and regulating stress.
Trait empathy	...capable of taking someone else's perspective.
Trait happiness	...cheerful and satisfied with their lives.
Trait optimism	...confident and likely to "look on the bright side" of life.

Adaptability

Change is inevitable in all aspects of life and there are no exceptions. It is essential for you to have the ability to adapt to changing situations. In order to adapt, you must first be able to make a clear distinction between what is preferred and what actually exists. You are unable to adapt to change that occurs when you are not first in touch with the reality of the specific situation. By the time your personal journey to renewal is complete, adaptability is something you will have mastered. This entire restoration process has been about change and once it is finished, there should be nothing about you (mind, body, or soul) that looks the same.

Our lives are constantly evolving and that is the beauty of it all. Adaptability helps us to successfully problem solve and attain our personal goals. Adaptability involves our willingness to be flexible and adjust behaviors, thoughts, and emotions to reflect the changing conditions. Also, reacting appropriately, quickly, and effectively to changes can minimize stress, discontent, and fear of the unknown. Most importantly, adaptability encompasses the ability to not only identify problems, but implement effective solutions that will counteract the problem. The sole purpose of this journey you are on is to simply restore you to greatness. While you've changed from the inside out, the same cannot be said for everyone or everything else. Your challenge now is to find your place in a world that looks differently from your new set of eyes. The world will not naturally conform to you. You must be intentional and proactive about the desires of your heart all while maintaining flexibility. Adaptability will serve as an umbrella to shield you from the inevitable storms of life.

Assertiveness

Often mistaken for being pushy and quite difficult for some individuals to do, being assertive is truly a core communication skill that is significantly beneficial in life. Having the ability to stand up for your own beliefs, thoughts and opinions yields effective self-expression. Being assertive can also help to boost self-confidence and help an individual gain respect from other people. Assertive people illustrate a willingness to stand up for their own rights and self-interests in a way that is respectful and direct. If you are honest with yourself prior to the beginning of your restoration process, you may have had difficulty expressing yourself or asserting yourself in situations that called for that type of response. The reason is because your view of "self" was different. Deep down you may have felt like you were not valuable enough to contribute an opposing opinion. Perhaps the negative self-talk you used to engage in so often convinced you that you were not worthy of self-advocacy. Once you have been restored to your original state of greatness, there will be no mistake about the fact that you are indeed a new creation. You will be able to readily identify your worth and the importance of always loving and protecting yourself.

Expression of Emotion

Another vitally important facet of Trait Emotional Intelligence is the expression of emotions. A significant part of being emotionally intelligent involves having the ability to communicate feelings to others whether non-verbal or verbal. The concept of emotional expression is quite historical and dates back to research done by Charles Darwin the early 1870s. Darwin's *The Expression in*

Man and Animals, was first published in 1872 and explored the facial expressions of emotions. Darwin gathered evidence and concluded that some emotions have respective facial expressions and that anyone with a significant absence of emotion was indicative of a mental condition. Darwin wrote: "Many idiots are morose, passionate, restless, in a painful state of mind, or utterly stolid and these never laugh [pg. 196]." In Darwin's view, absence of expression illustrated dysfunction and the individual's inability to truly be present in life's process.

Having the ability to express your feelings is one of life's wonderful gifts. Create, maintain, and submerge yourself in environments that promote open communication and help to facilitate the expression of emotions. Any person, place, or thing that causes you to hide your true feelings or mask genuine emotion should be avoided at all costs. Now that you've done the hard work to re-discover yourself, you have a responsibility to protect the new and improved "you". You matter. Express yourself!

Management of Emotion

Hochschild (1983) created the term "emotion management" to refer to an individual's efforts to make their own emotions correspond to those required by situational expectations. Managing the emotions of self and others is a core component of trait Emotional Intelligence. In order to manage the emotions of other people, it is first necessary to be able to identify emotions. Empathy, social awareness, and self-awareness must be present in order to begin to understand the feelings of self as well as others. Some people may possess the ability to identify other people's emotions. However, their personal responsibilities often make it increasingly difficult to take time to *care* about how others are feeling. This ability is undoubtedly beneficial because relationships you build throughout life are essential to your personal growth. The relationships will either help to catapult you to a sphere of greatness or significantly hold you back. The emotionally intelligent individual understands the importance of an equal exchange. Do everything in your power to ensure that you engaging in interdependent relationships.

The individual with emotional intelligence is also socially aware and can manage the emotions of other people. This is not to imply emotional intelligence is solely about controlling other people. Trait Emotional Intelligence affords competencies that allow people to manage their own emotions directly, which can indirectly influence outcomes when considering the emotions of other people. The idea behind management of emotion is that it is a skill through which we learn to treat emotions as valuable data that can assist in navigation through certain situations. A specific example could be an individual that has the ability to perceive the emotions and behaviors of another person. Therefore, that person knows when it is best to engage in communication that will lead to favorable outcomes. Let's say you have an excellent idea to share, an in depth conversation you need to have, or an issue that needs resolution. However, you know the person you need to communicate with tends to be irritable and short-tempered in the morning. Emotional intelligence allows you to assess the situation, regulate your emotions, curb the excitement of the moment, and wait for the most opportune time to approach the other party. Knowing *what* to say in a given situation is just as important as knowing *when* to say it.

Perception of Emotion

Generally, most people believe they have the ability to read emotions in other people. It is often assumed that an individual's behavior, language, or facial expression is a manifestation of their current emotional state. Many of us tend to actively explore facial expressions in order to recognize emotions. Perception of emotion involves the ability to both recognize and interpret our own feelings as well as others. This goes a step past acknowledging the presence of an emotion and shifting gears to understand what the emotion means and how it should be interpreted. Perception is defined as: "the way you think about or understand someone or something."

An individual's perceptions are influenced by personal beliefs and expectations brought to the given situation. The ability to perceive emotions in oneself and others entails identifying internal signals of emotional experience and emotional information in facial expressions or tone of voice. Emotional intelligence helps you to choose the best course of action when navigating through social situations. For example, the ability to decipher facial expressions of emotion can help to evaluate how other people may respond to your words and actions. This will yield important information that may call for adjustment of any future behavior.

Regulation of Emotion

Through the regulation of emotions, you are able to control what emotions you have, the actual experience of the emotions, and most importantly control your outward expression of these emotions. At some point throughout your lifespan you've heard someone say, "there is a time and place for everything." Regulation of emotion is critical when relationship building. It is important to note that regulation of emotion does not mean suppression of all emotions that are not positive. Negative emotions are inevitable and they too must be validated, recognized, and accepted as real and significant. However, it is important to truly understand that your emotions will drive your behavior. Make it a priority to reduce vulnerability to negative emotions, which can drive undesirable behaviors such as outbursts, arguments, or physical altercations. Why does any of this matter to you? Your ability to regulate your emotions will make all the difference as you are building new relationships. Whether a personal or professional relationship, no one wants to spend any significant amount of time around someone who lacks self-control. Learn to say what you mean, mean what you say, and above all else make sure you are representing your "best" self while doing so. It takes significant amounts of time to build solid relationships. On the other hand, it takes one argument, outburst, or mismanagement of emotion to ruin the foundation of that relationship.

Impulsiveness

Being emotionally intelligent requires an individual to have the ability to cognitively process situations thoroughly before taking certain courses of action. Impulsive behaviors are emotionally driven and can be irrational because consequences have not been considered. Impulsive behavior is dangerous and relationships that took years to build can be destroyed in minutes as a result. Research has shown that individuals with trait emotional intelligence are less likely to engage in impulsivity.

Every step of your life will not be planned out. The truth is that life is far more beautiful because there are so many components we cannot plan or control. Some of our most amazing life experiences come when we least expect them as a result of being impulsive and seizing the moment. Being emotionally intelligent does not mean you become a robot void of emotion and unable to just enjoy life as it comes. Emotional intelligence does not prohibit you from expressing yourself. It is quite the opposite actually. Being emotionally intelligent simply means you are more in control while expressing your emotions. It means you are no longer willing to give into the temptation of reacting faster than your brain can process the situation. Emotional intelligence requires the ability to engage in a real thought process in conjunction with your emotions. It is the marriage of emotion and intelligence.

Relationship Skills

Many life success stories depend on an individual's ability to build and maintain strong relationships. Strong relationships are built over time and are made up of trust and dependability. Emotional intelligence provides a person with the ability to understand the difference between effective and non-effective communication. It also allows us to transform conflict into more positive opportunities for relationship building. Whether verbal or nonverbal, communication is key to any successful relationship. Solid relationships will ultimately graduate to a point where there is shared meaning and understanding behind a particular look or gesture. It is an amazing feeling to have a relationship with someone who truly knows and accepts you; flaws and all.

All relationships are not created equally. Some relationships happen quite naturally, while others take considerably more effort. Your only responsibility is to make sure you are open to experiencing new relationships as long as they are mutually beneficial. Long gone are the days where you engage in one-sided friendships, business or personal partnerships. Now that you are on your way to being fully restored, you must know the importance of maintaining fulfilling relationships. There is absolutely no need to keep people around who do not edify you in any way. Emotional intelligence will enhance your relationship building skill sets and ensure that you are not only creating relationships, but that they are rewarding.

Self-Esteem

Self-esteem has been described as the affective or evaluative appraisal of self; basically how much a person likes or dislikes themselves. Self-esteem is an important attribute that can either significantly enhance or impede an individual's overall success in life. In order to truly be emotionally intelligent, one must be in tune with self. Research has suggested that higher emotional intelligence is associated with high self-esteem. How people feel about themselves is often indicative of how they feel about others. Only after first learning to like yourself can you genuinely begin to like others.

Have you experienced being around a person who never has anything nice to say? There is no need to name names. We all know at least one person and quite frankly that "one" may be you! The best way to identify an individual's level of self-esteem is by taking notice of how insistent they are on belittling other people. When you genuinely know and like yourself, you more closely identify with the best parts of you and will tend to see that in other people.

Conversely, when you don't care for yourself and are battling self-esteem issues, you will easily identify poor characteristics in others that *you* have. While you are so busy judging others, what you are actually doing is judging yourself. The reason why you can so easily identify his/her "bad attitude" is likely because *you* have one. The reason why you so are so quick to criticize his/her outer appearance is because you likely have issues with the way *you* look.

Your restoration experience is not only about returning to your original state of greatness, but enhancing your awareness of that greatness. When you live a life that expresses your understanding of just how significant you are, you unknowingly give other people permission to be phenomenal as well. You will know for certain your restoration journey is near completion when you genuinely know and love who you are; including your flaws. When you can be candid about who you are and know for sure it is always good enough, you will begin to draw the *right* people into your space of authenticity.

Many of the relationships you were involved in prior to your restoration journey were the direct result of your low self-esteem. Some of you knew it was time to end the relationship and simply couldn't because you believed you were unworthy of better. Now that you know beyond a shadow of a doubt that you are worth every good thing your heart desires, your relationships will begin to look and feel completely different. You will attract to you people who also love themselves and want to be around the positive energy that you are emitting. Being surrounded by the types of people who genuinely want to see you do well in life will provide ongoing opportunities to obtain new levels of self-awareness. It is their pleasure to edify and build you up! They will hold you accountable and do everything within their power to help you keep your appointment with destiny!

When you feel good about yourself, you exude a radiance from the inside out that is both invaluable and untouchable. Not to be confused with arrogance or conceit, your self-esteem will prohibit you from engaging in negative self-talk. You'll know for certain there is no task too complex, no goal unattainable, and no good thing of which you are undeserving. When your self-esteem is in order, you are more likely to take risks and welcome challenges in life because you truly believe in your ability to handle whatever may come.

Self-Motivation

A significant part of being emotionally intelligent requires self-motivation. Self-motivation is our ability to attain a particular goal without being influenced by someone else to do so. What motivates you? If honest, you can admit you've spent significant amounts of time being motivated by things other than your own intrinsic desires. Some of you have spent years being motivated by the desire to change someone's opinion of you. People will always have their own ideas and perceptions about who you are. Once you are truly restored, your mind, body, and spirit will fully reject the idea of being motivated through fear of being misjudged by other people. Your ability to be self-motivated will only come when you have a clear-cut definition of who you are. To know and love yourself will then open the door to the possibility of discovering what you truly want from life separate of any external motivators.

Social Competence

Social competence encompasses a number of factors including social skills, social awareness, and self-confidence. Social competence describes the ability to distinguish and use social behaviors that are appropriate to a given situation. It is ever changing, depending solely on the individual and their current environment. Like chameleons, socially competent individuals are able to blend in successfully regardless of the setting. Social competence can help establish and maintain both high quality and mutually satisfying relationships.

Social competency is highly important as you branch out and meet new people. Please do not mistake social competence for conformity. No one is requiring you to blend in so much with your immediate surroundings that there is failure to consistently display your own individuality. Social competence encourages you to be able to revel in the beauty of diversity while actively engaging in a cohesive environment. Plainly put, you must know how to engage people. More than that, you must get to a place where you understand there is value in opposing views. As a student of life, you must always be open to learning from other people. There will be certain people who enter your life with the sole purpose of teaching you a valuable lesson your Creator needs you to learn at that particular time.

Stress management

Dr. Hans Selye (1956) defined stress as "the nonspecific response of the body to any demand made upon it." The "demand" can be a perceived threat, challenge or any form of change that requires the body to adapt. Stress is inevitable but individuals who are capable of withstanding pressure and regulating stress are more likely to find life more satisfying. The reason is because even in the face of adversity, those who have mastered the ability to handle stress will find value in the situation. There is always a lesson to be learned from any trials you are presented throughout life. It won't necessarily be the absence of stress that contributes to the quality of your life. It will be your resolve and unwavering commitment to the management of stress that makes all the difference.

Authored by American theologian Reinhold Niebuhr, the serenity prayer reminds us that there is power in accepting things we cannot change, having courage to change what we can, and wisdom to identify the difference between the two situations. As you press forward and begin to rebuild your network of relationships both personal and professional, you must choose wisely. Stress is not something you can avoid altogether throughout life. However, the relationships you choose to be part of should all be enriching, mutually beneficial, and free of any ongoing stress. If your relationships do not fit the above criteria, then it is highly likely they are not meant to be.

In the past, many of you have experienced one poor relationship after the other. While each of those relationships stripped you of something valuable, your restoration period has given it all back and more! Emotional intelligence gives you all of the tools necessary to build and manage healthy relationships with yourself and others. You are now equipped and ready to press toward the finish line knowing for certain that you and only you are in control of the relationships in your life. **All of your personal and professional relationships must EDIFY: Encourage your Development and Ignite the Fire in You!** You have a date with destiny and if you intend to keep your appointment, it will require utmost strategy in relationship selectivity. The relationships you form will either serve as a vehicle to help get you there or a variety of roadblocks prohibiting your divine appointment. The choice is yours!

Prayer:

Lord, help me to consistently manage healthy relationships in my life. Help me to discern when you have put the right people in my life at the right time. Give me the strength I need to be able to cut off any relationships that are not in alignment with the direction in which my life is going. Help me to understand there is nothing wrong with loving and caring for people from afar. Most importantly, help me to remember the importance of being able to manage my emotions while building new friendships, business partnerships, and yes—a new love relationship! Amen.

CHAPTER 12: REFLECTIONS

Emotional Intelligence (EI) is a relatively new concept, but one that will inevitably keep you on track to success! Answer the following questions:

1. According to the Mayer and Salovey Trait EI Model, what are the 4 types of EI abilities?

_____

_____

_____

2. Which of the Trait Emotional Intelligence facets resonated most with you and why?

_____

_____

_____

3. Now that you've read Chapter 12 in its entirety and have been introduced to Emotional Intelligence, on a scale of 1-10—how emotionally intelligent would you rate yourself? Why?

_____

_____

_____

CHAPTER 13: REVELATIONS

By its original definition, 'revelation' is the uncovering, removal of a veil, or disclosure of what was once unknown. In essence, revelation is often the tool used by God to make himself known to His people. Everything you will come to know about God and ultimately yourself throughout this process will be through revelation. Get ready for the next level of understanding because it will literally blow your mind. There is nothing more powerful than the feeling you have immediately after a revelation. For months or (in some cases) years you have been desperately trying to fit the pieces of the puzzle together. All of a sudden in what would seem like out of nowhere, you begin to see and hear certain things that will somehow answer many of your questions. Having a revelation can be compared to going from blurry to 20/20 vision. It is as though you are viewing life through a new lens and are now able to see things more clearly than ever. It will feel as though you are now in possession of missing clues to what used to be an unsolved mystery.

As you have been moving throughout the restoration process, there have been plenty of moments when you've asked "why". Until now, you may not have received the answers you were desperately seeking. It is easy to give up hope and resign yourself to never truly getting the closure you need as a result of so many unanswered questions. However, God sees all and waited until He could be certain you were mature enough to handle the answers and utilize them for self- empowerment. There are some questions God will answer for you in due time. There are other answers you may never receive and you must be ok with that fact. In those cases, the "why" just simply wasn't as important as the "what" to God. Why He allowed you to experience a specific hardship will pale in comparison to the importance of "what" lesson He intended for you to learn!

Be prepared for the downpour of revelation. Revelations almost never comes one at a time. They will come fast and furious so make sure you are ready. You will surely be overwhelmed as God reveals the "whys" and "hows" of it all. The revealing of this valuable information will serve as a key to unlock doors that once prohibited you from navigating freely. You will be impressed by the sheer genius of the timing in which certain things are revealed to you. It is impossible to experience revelation and not be able to recognize God hard at work right along with you during your restoration process.

VIEW REVELATION AS THE BLESSING AND GIFT THAT IT IS TO YOU.

It is extremely important that you never take revelation for granted. You are being given answers so that you can have a more profound understanding of certain situations that have happened. You must intentionally utilize this knowledge to help you going forward. Revelation will inevitably assist you in better decision making if you allow the information to permeate your spirit and guide you in the right direction. The most essential thing to remember is to always remain in a frame of mind that is receptive to what the Lord is trying to reveal to you.

Certain things in life will be revealed while others are not. However, you can be sure God will not leave a question mark where there should be a period. He will always provide you with exactly what you need and when you need it in order for you to move forward in your restoration process. That being said, what you need may not always be what you want. You must be mature enough to know the difference. There will be some situations in which you never experience revelation but closure *is* achieved through forgiveness and surrender. In those instances, all you need to know is that God cannot make mistakes. Believe with your whole heart that whatever took place had to happen in order to help usher you into your greatness. If you give it the credit it deserves, you will find (although hurtful) that specific situation has actually helped to bring about a change in interests, attitudes, mindsets, and/or overall character in you. It worked out for your good and therefore the "why" of it all is irrelevant.

Revelation will come in all different shapes and forms. It may come in the way of a dream, as you read in the book of Daniel, during the 21 days of his fast when God communicated information through dreams. Many fast for guidance when facing a major, life-changing decision. Some fast for help in a specific area, and some fast and pray for other people that are facing tough situations. Your personal reasoning for fasting is all your own.

There was one particular period of fasting that was incredibly life-changing for me. Prior to the fast, I prayed and told God exactly what I wanted to know from Him. For 21 days I fasted, prayed, and kept detailed notes of my dreams. By the third day of the fast, my spirit was starting to feel quite unsettled. I was able to recognize the development of a pattern in my dreams. It was becoming increasingly clearer that God was uninterested in revealing what I *wanted* to know. Instead, He was fixed on revealing what I *needed* to know. I'd asked Him to reveal my purpose, His plan for a possible husband/children, and what I should do about various broken relationships with family and former friends. God had something altogether different in mind.

He chose to reveal some of my most deeply embedded character flaws and in doing so, explain *why*:

- I was not in alignment with my purpose (disobedient and fearful)
- I was not *ready* for a husband or children (mentally, physically, and spiritually out of order)
- I had so many broken relationships (resentful, angry, and bitter)

That period of fasting was extremely difficult for me. To be most candid, as the days went by, I felt myself becoming more and more frustrated. The detail of each dream was confusing because they (at first) seemed to have nothing to do with what I'd asked God to reveal to me. In this specific instance, I had to first have a revelation about the *purpose* of what God was revealing to me at that time. Once that fast was completed and I was able to review what I'd learned, I realized the complete and undeniable perfectness of God. This fast wasn't about revealing to me how, when, or if I would ever receive the desires of my heart. It was about revealing to me why I had yet to attain them! At that particular time in my life God was intent on showing me that it was I who was (quite unintentionally) blocking my *own* flow of blessings. There is nothing more powerful than a divine revelation at the right time! In the words of the great Maya Angelou, "When we know better, we do better!"

BE READY TO TAKE ADVANTAGE OF REVELATION IN ANY WAY THAT IT COMES TO BLESS YOU.

Revelation may also come from those closest to you. Our loved ones are close enough to us to know what is going on in our lives and offer the support we need at any given time. They can also be far enough removed to offer an objective point of view. Sometimes when we are deeply entrenched in a given situation, our judgment is significantly impaired. The people closest to you will be able to draw from their vantage point and use the objectivity to empower you. An aerial view is always different from on the ground. As long as you are open to the possibility that revelation may come from engaging in conversation with people who are not directly connected to the situation, you are less likely to miss the opportunity to learn something very important.

During this process you will come to know new depths and breadths of yourself that you've never before experienced. God will use other people to show you characteristics about yourself that are hindering you from living your best life. Please don't be too shocked if that one coworker or supervisor that continuously rubs you the wrong way has actually been sent to teach you a valuable lesson about yourself. On the other hand, God may also use people to inspire you and awaken aspirations that had been rocked to sleep through the years. He can show you that what you've been dreaming about all these years is actually possible. For example, perhaps you are contemplating going back to college to complete your degree. While you are excited about the possibility of finally finishing something you started, you are also fearful that you're too old and have waited too long. That is, until you muster up enough courage to attend an interest session at the college/university of your choice. It is there that you just happen to meet a 62 year old recent graduate of the program you plan to enter. During that information session she speaks candidly about her past fears of returning back to the classroom. Most importantly she affirms faith, hard work, and the support of an amazing faculty helped her attain this personal goal. The beautiful thing about revelation is that God can and will often bring you face to face with a live example of what you desire. The purpose is to illustrate that the goals you seek to attain are more than feasible. Sometimes revelation comes on the wings of an angel with the sole purpose of increasing our individual levels of self-awareness and activating our fatigued faith muscles.

For the first time in your life you will truly understand who you are, why certain life experiences happened, why certain friendships have withstood the test of time, why certain relationships didn't last, and how all of these things have worked together to prepare you for this very moment in life.

While experiencing different revelations throughout the process you will be able to put all of the pieces together. It will begin to make sense to you why this relationship happened and what you were supposed to learn as a result. No longer is this experience something you mentally label as "just" a breakup. You now recognize it as a tool used by God to bring you to a place of submission and begin a process that would forever change your life. You are stronger than you ever thought possible. You are wiser than you ever thought possible. You are more compassionate than ever, thus revealing your freedom from the stronghold of bitterness. You are more self-aware and capable of decision making that most benefits you physically, emotionally, and spiritually. While all of these revelations are working within to help you transform into a new creature, none will compare to the arrival of the "big reveal".

The "Big Reveal" is when you once and for all learn the definition of love as spoken to your spirit by God. Many of us are familiar with the definition of love that we've read time and again in the Bible. In 1 Corinthians 13:4 we read, "Love is patient, love is kind; love does not envy; love does not parade itself, is not puffed up; does not behave rudely, does not seek its own, is not provoked, seeks no evil, does not rejoice in iniquity, but rejoices in truth; bears all things, believes all things, hopes all things, endures all things. Love never fails." If we are honest with ourselves, we can admit that by God's definition, many of us have never experienced that kind of love in our lifetime. However, you must know beyond a shadow of a doubt that is exactly the kind of love God provides and what He wants for you in your relationships.

The true meaning of love as found in the Bible has been corrupted in the common usage of our English language and society. Most often, love is confused with infatuation, which is that "high" or elated feeling we get while falling in love. This is the kind of "love" has an expiration date and often results in broken relationships. The Bible indicates that love is from God. In fact, the Bible says, "God *is* love."[1] Love is one of the primary characteristics of God. Likewise, God has endowed us with the capacity for love, since we are created in His image.

There are all different kinds of love. In the language of the New Testament there are two different words used to describe and define love. The most commonly used Greek word for "love" in the New Testament is "agape." This type of love is a representation of God's love for you. It is an unconditional, sacrificial love probably best represented by God's decision to send humanity a Savior. In John 3:16 we read, "For God so loved (agape) the world, that He gave His only begotten Son, that whoever believes in Him should not perish, but have eternal life." Regardless of who we are or how far we've fallen from grace, God's love is unconditional.

In contrast, "love" as we know it is quite different because we view it as only a feeling, a fleeting emotion. The problem with "falling into" love is that we can just as easily fall out of it. We identify love as something conditional and dependent upon how other people behave toward us. On the other hand, agape love gives, sacrifices, and expects nothing in return. It is powerful beyond measure and once you are truly able to adopt the full meaning of the word "love" as defined by God you will be able to feel that power and draw that caliber of love into your life.

The "Big Reveal" isn't just about providing you with God's true definition of love. The most important revelation you can have while going through your restoration process is arriving at the understanding of how powerful love is. Love is a gift from God and it is how we as His children give Him glory each day. When we love, we are able to transcend and elevate above any and all circumstances life may bring. This is why the enemy seeks to pervert the one most important thing God created to edify and uplift His people. What better way to rob you of the opportunity to live the life God intended for you? If we are uncertain of and lack true definition of what real love is, then we become vulnerable to counterfeit relationships comprised of lust and/or infatuation.

AS HUMAN BEINGS WE SEEK TO LOVE AND BE LOVED.

The late Dr. Maya Angelou has been quoted as saying, "We are more alike than we are different." The truth is that regardless of age, race, gender or any other demographic that is used to help highlight our differences, we are all the same. This must have indeed been God's truest intention. However, the problem is that many are searching high and low for a validation of significance that can only come from within. Sometimes we need to know other people "love" us before we can commit to loving ourselves and therein lies the biggest problem of all. Many of us don't know what true love is, have yet to experience it, and are therefore have a difficult time giving it to others. Know this: **Relationships are mirrors.** At any given time you can assess your relationship with self by the relationships you have with other people. Whether you realize it or not, every day of your life you are showing people how to treat you by how you treat yourself. Love yourself and in doing so, give an unspoken mandate for the very same reflection of love from others.

God is the ultimate creator of all things. The enemy cannot create; he can only modify and/or change what has already been created. In the Book of Job, the text literally illustrates the devil asking for God's *permission* to harm Job. Have you ever considered the fact that the enemy can do absolutely nothing without God's permission? In 1 Peter 5:8, the word reminds us to "Be alert and of sober mind. Your enemy, the devil prowls around like a roaring lion looking for someone to devour." It is the enemy's sole task to take everything that God has created to empower us and use it for destruction. God created love to build His people, drawing us nearer to each other and Himself. The enemy attempted to use this past relationship of yours to help plant doubt about the power of God's greatest gift. Once you become someone who no longer believes in love or its power, you become ineffective for the advancement of God's Kingdom. You can do absolutely nothing for God or His people without love. Your knowledge of what true love is will empower you to make significantly better decisions regarding your future relationships.

Ignorance is to blame for why there are so many Christians walking the earth brokenhearted, bitter, angry, emotionally bankrupt and virtually useless for the kingdom of God. Love is the single most powerful shield God has created to help you on the battlefield of life. Love is cyclical. God provides an overflow of unconditional love that allows us to be able to give it away to others. It is your responsibility to always make sure God's definition of love is the criterion for each of your relationships. The promotion of anything less than that definition can be classified as fraudulence. Keep in mind the same way God is able to hear our prayers, so is the devil. The enemy is fully aware of the desires of your heart as expressed while deep in prayer. He knows that you long to love and be loved. He knows how long you've been waiting. He knows the "type" you normally go for and when the most opportune time is to send the wrong person your way. Your counterfeit "love" will almost always look and feel like everything you've ever wanted. You wouldn't exactly tempt an alcoholic with food. There is no point in attempting to get you off track with someone that would not appeal to you. Make no mistake, whatever you seek most in a mate, your counterfeit "love" *will have it*!

If your self-esteem is an issue, your counterfeit will come on a white horse whispering all of the sweet words you've been longing to hear someone say to you. If you are financially unstable, your counterfeit will appear to be your ticket out of the fiscally irresponsible mess you've created. If aesthetics are most important, your counterfeit will be the finest man/woman you've ever seen! You will be presented with the individual that seems to have what you value most. Without the "Big Reveal" and ongoing communication with your heavenly father, you will likely not be able to accurately discern the deceit until it is too late. This is precisely how you ended up emotionally, physically, mentally broken and in need of restoration.

The reason why so many of us are weakened and susceptible to falling for the wrong person is because until we are restored, we lack the invaluable knowledge of our true identities. Our individual, personal relationships with God must be strengthened through an ongoing, consistent prayer life. When there is a breakdown in that essential line of communication, we are left unable to discern which relationships have been sent from the Lord and which are simply distractions. Establish and maintain God's definition of love in your relationships to avoid the enemy's craftily designed pitfalls with the sole intention of destroying your faith in God's greatest gift to you: **LOVE**.

As Christians we must seek to both understand and embody God's definition of love. God's love is perfect and you will never find an exact replication of it in any human being. That is an impossible feat and you should therefore refrain from entertaining that ideal. Rather, learn to use your revelation of what love is to help you navigate through your next relationship. The relationship won't be perfect, but there should absolutely be semblances of God's love in it! Is this individual patient with you? Is this person humble? Is this person dependable? Is this individual kind? Is this individual selfless? Those are all questions you will need to ask yourself when the time comes. Remember to always use God's definition of love as your gauge.

Most importantly, you should be able to ask and answer this very important question: "Given my personal relationship with God and all He has revealed to me, do I genuinely believe this is the relationship designed for me?" There must be a resounding "yes" from the depths of your soul regarding any/all relationships in your life. Lacking that internal affirmation is all the indication you need to end the relationship, redefine the relationship, or refrain from entering it altogether. The entire restoration process is about you and your relationship with God. As you near the end of your season, there will be no doubt your relationship with God has become more intimate than you could have ever imagined. You will be on a first name basis and able to hear from Him like never before. This journey of self-discovery has taught you the importance of patience and waiting for revelation before making major life decisions.

Once you have experienced your own personal "Big Reveal" you will know for sure your restoration process is nearing its end. You view "love" completely differently now and understand unequivocally that it is a gift directly from God. If you ever find yourself in a relationship that is void of God's presence, then it is not love. You will know exactly what to do at that very moment in time. You have been forever empowered to give and receive real love. Do not let anyone convince you that the standards and expectations set for your relationships are unreasonable. Who says you deserve to be loved unconditionally? God says so!

Prayer:

Thank you Lord for the "Big Reveal". It is by your grace alone that I now know for sure what true love is! Thank you for loving me unconditionally through all of my flaws. I am imperfectly perfected in you and am deserving of relationships that reflect your presence. When I am faced with relationships that feel uncertain please grant me the gift of discernment. Help me to never get ahead of you and to always remember to apply your definition of love to each of my relationships.

CHAPTER 13: REFLECTIONS

The 'Big Reveal' is God's definition of "love". Once you truly know and operate from God's definition of love, your life will never be the same again. Take some time to answer the following questions derived from Chapter 13.

1. **After reading Chapter 13, how has your definition of true love changed?**

   _____

   _____

   _____

2. **Describe a situation in your life where you were certain everything happening was far from coincidence. How did you handle the revelation that came from the experience?**

   _____

   _____

   _____

3. **How is God's love different from the love of a mate in your opinion?**

   _____

   _____

   _____

CHAPTER 14: RESTORED

The word restoration is defined in many different ways, however each definition of the word is conceptually applicable to the process you will experience. Restoration is defined as the act of returning something back to its original condition by repairing it, cleaning it, etc. We've mentioned restoration throughout the entire book, but until now didn't go into detail about *what* is being restored. This entire process is about restoring you, the broken vessel, to your original state of greatness as created by God. It is far more intricate than the simple healing of a broken heart. As you go deeper into the restoration process it will become evident there are other areas of you that are broken and need repair. To fix the heart but not the mind would be pointless. A healed heart connected to a broken mind can only yield much of the same behaviors. The journey cannot be complete until the who, what, when, where *and* why of your specific situations have been addressed. True restoration will yield a healed heart, a revelation of your authentic self, and a heightened spirituality by the rigorous exercising of your faith muscle.

The word restoration can also be used to describe the act of returning something that was stolen or taken. Another significant objective of this process is to give back all that had been stolen from you. Joy, peace, love, and understanding were all intangible things that were stolen from you as a result of the ended relationship. The heartbreak you experienced left you in a state of confusion, bitterness, and on the verge of losing faith in love; which is the most powerful gift given to us by God. Complete restoration ensures you will be victorious in reclaiming all that belongs to you. But first, you'll need to take small steps of faith toward the one, unchanging source of Agape love and stay in His presence long enough to receive renewal.

There are significant changes that will occur throughout your individual season of restoration. If you are anything like me, you are most interested to know what signs to look for in order to confirm all of the necessary changes are taking place. While there will be countless changes, some will be subtle while others are extremely obvious to you and others. Below is a simple list of some of the changes you should look forward to experiencing as a result of a completed restoration process:

1. **Your thought patterns will be significantly different.** Prior to this extensive personal development, your thought pattern was in direct correlation with the state of your heart; broken, battered, and bruised. Your thought life was pessimistic and you scowled at the thought of happiness. Happiness was an incredibly foreign concept and felt almost impossible for you to every experience again. However, once you have been restored, you will be able to readily identify a change in the way you think. Your thoughts will be filled with hope, joy, and possibility. Your thought life will wholeheartedly embody Philippians 4:13 "I can do all things through Christ who strengthens me." You will be able to stop negative thought patterns from forming and use your faith to destroy fear in every area your life.

2. **Your relationship with God will be at an unprecedented level of understanding.** Your relationship will have grown tremendously and you will truly understand He is the very reason for your being. You now know that He must be incorporated into every aspect of your life. You will be extremely hesitant to make any major decisions in your life without the counsel of the Holy Spirit. You'll now recognize that haste, in conjunction with your lack of a relationship with God is what contributed to the dilapidated state of your mind, body, and spirit prior to the restoration process.

3. **Your close circle will change drastically.** You will see people you believed were friends for life have come and gone. As you got closer to God, you found certain people falling by the wayside for what seemed like no real significant reason. What you now understand is that God was calling you out from among all of the others. God is sovereign enough to know that you will only go as far as the people with whom you surround yourself. These changes came about throughout the process because as you got to know yourself better, your knowledge of God was greatly enhanced. Your spirit was able to recognize a need to be around like-minded, positive individuals whose lives are all going in a positive direction. Your newfound wisdom will not allow you to share time and space with people who are negative and aren't on the same page as you. You will appropriately categorize these types of relationships as a waste of valuable time.

4. **Your personality will change.** That is not to imply this process mirrors the invasion of the body snatchers. There will absolutely still be characteristics about yourself that you are able to readily identify. However, there will also be significant differences. Long gone are the bitterness, anger, aggression, and/or depression that came along with the end of your relationship. Your aura will be one of completion, joy, peace,

and self-awareness. You will be more compassionate than ever before and have grown to possess a genuine affinity for people. At this point you have self-actualized and realize you are here on earth with the sole purpose of serving others in whatever capacity God has ordained. You will be covered by a glow of humility and servitude wherever you go. Life will have a deeper meaning for you! There will be an audacity about you that even those closest to you cannot recognize. You have learned to come boldly to the throne of grace to ask for the desires of you heart. You have learned to press past fear and embrace your faith during times of adversity. All that you have experienced has served to make you stronger than ever before and it will *show*!

5.   **You will begin to attract a different caliber of people into your life**. This is not solely restricted to your potential significant other. This includes all of your relationships whether personal or professional. Don't be surprised if someone you have worked with for a significant amount of time begins to take notice in the changes that are manifesting in you. People will respond to you and your presence in a way that you've never experienced before. You will encounter a shift of divine favor and observe people go out of their way to support you. The "type" that was once attracted to you will no longer approach you. The reason for this is because everything in you that they once identified with has been purged. Angry people won't want to be around you because your joy will overshadow their negativity. Fearful people will not want to be in relationships with you because your faith will be something they genuinely can't relate to or understand. Deceitful people will steer clear of you because your honesty and love of truth will make them extremely uncomfortable.

6. **Your physical self will inevitably begin to change as well.** The reason for this is because you are now more self-aware than ever before. Your knowledge of who you are, what you want, and what you are worth are all working together to empress upon your spirit the importance of loving self and taking care of the temple God has given you. You will value your body in a way that you never thought possible. You will ensure healthy eating habits, physical exercise, and time allotted for prayer/meditation. You will find yourself making an extra effort to incorporate things you love to do, that enhance your sense of well-being into your schedule. As all of these components work together, you will begin to look and feel good about yourself. In Psalm 139:14, David says to God, "I praise you because I am fearfully and wonderfully made; your works are wonderful, I know that full well." You will finally see yourself as God sees you! Fearfully and wonderfully made in His likeness and powerful beyond measure.

7. **Your ability to discern the voice of God will be phenomenal.** You will no longer be confused about if certain relationships were sent to you from God or the adversary. You will be directly in tune with the Spirit of God. You will always know for sure what is genuine and what is counterfeit. This ability will help you to avoid potentially disastrous situations with ease. As a result, you will know when to back off and let certain "opportunities" pass by versus when to step up and seize the moment. This newly activated "inside track" will help assist you during the most important decisions you make in life.

In 2 Corinthians 5:17, the Word of God reminds us, "Therefore if any man be in Christ, he is a new creature; old things are passed away; behold all things are become new." This scripture is being used to remind you that as a Christian, belonging to Christ gives you the right to restoration. You have the right to present yourself to God regardless of flaws and by faith, with great expectancy, be renewed. You are entitled to restitution, hope, and a life full of limitless possibilities. As a new creation, your spirit will naturally reject everything that is reminiscent of whom you used to be!

TRUE RESTORATION WILL YIELD A HEALED HEART

Similar to the restoration of furniture, the most important thing to note is that the process itself is lengthy. If a finished product just shy of perfection is what you intend to accomplish, there can be no hastening of the process. Each step is deliberate, purposeful and all work together to create a masterpiece. The irony of restoration is the understanding of the fact that the "piece" being restored was *already* invaluable. Weather conditions, mistreatment, and misuse may have altered the outer appearance of that particular piece of furniture. However, its original quality and value could not be altered. In fact, we can even venture to say that if the product was not of value, there would be no purpose in even attempting to restore it! That is how God views you! In the beginning, He created nothing short of a masterpiece.

In Psalm 139, David illustrates his understanding of God's infinite wisdom. David wrote, "You have searched me, Lord and you know me. You know when I sit and when I rise; you perceive my thoughts from afar. Before a word is on my tongue, you know it completely. Where can I go from your spirit? Where can I flee from your presence?" This particular Psalm is indeed powerful because it reminds us of God's both omniscience *and* omnipotence. He knows all of the circumstances that have happened to you over time. He is also fully aware of how those situations have contributed to reshaping and altering of your physical, mental, and spiritual composition. However, what God knows for sure is that those experiences do not define you and can never alter or modify the complete and perfected being He originally created. He has searched you, and knows everything about you and even in the most wretched condition you can still be restored to greatness!

One of the first steps taken in the restoration process is to **strip** the furniture and remove the hardware. The "hardware" represents any and everything attached to the furniture piece that would in any way inhibit a complete and perfected finish. In your case, the "hardware" was your past relationships. God saw fit to remove you from people who were not prospering you; holding you back from being your very best self. The stripping process was painful but truly necessary as restoration requires you to be uncovered and in your original condition. In this case, your original state is bare, vulnerable and yet perfect in God's sight.

It is important to further explore this step in the process because there is significant meaning behind it! It is human nature to feel most vulnerable when naked or unclothed. Yet although being fully exposed is when we are most uncomfortable, it is also the only way to establish what areas are flawed and need correction. While the stripping process is not the most painful in the process, it may often be the most shocking to the system. The stripping away of almost everything relatively normal and comfortable to you can cause you to feel like life as you know it is over. There are certain components of your life that have consistently worked together to create a foundation. The idea of separation from those elements will yield anxiety due to uncertainty of what the future holds. What you must know for sure is that this step is not optional. The process of restoration cannot begin until the hardware is removed and you are separated from people, places, and things that restrict your ability to be transparent with self.

The second step in the restoration process is **sanding**. The purpose here is to smooth out all of the rough edges that came as a result of the stripping process. After you were stripped of your relationship, anger and bitterness began to settle into your heart. The sanding process involves God using the necessary tools to level out your emotions and bring you back to a place where you were open to experiencing joy again. Your relationship with God will grow stronger during this particular phase. Your knowledge of self will be enhanced. Your ability to express yourself in prayer and take faith-based risks will be evident. And finally, your thought life will inevitably change during the sanding process. Every rough edge and every unsightly piece of you will begin to transform into something smooth and ready for the next level.

Be prepared for the fact that it may be the sanding process that will feel most painful to you. You may be saying to yourself, "Knowledge of self, a better prayer life, faith based-risks, and renewed thought life sound pretty easy..." In the wise words of abolitionist Frederick Douglass, "without struggle, there can be no progress." The sanding phase of restoration will be full of struggle both internally and externally.

- In order to gain access to a higher level of self-knowledge you have to be willing to accept the fact that you will learn things about yourself that you do not like. You will undoubtedly come face to face with characteristics of yourself that may make you want to run and hide. You will struggle to be honest with yourself and admit there are ways about you that require immediate change.

- To have a better prayer life you will struggle in the process of yielding to your spirit. There will be times when you will be awakened at 1, 2, or possible 3 in the morning and your spirit will instruct you to pray. You will not understand it at first and more than likely you will force yourself to ignore it and go back to sleep. The struggle comes as you learn to be obedient. Your arms are in fact too short to box with God. To obtain His blessings, you must eventually yield to His will. The number of rounds in the boxing ring will be entirely up to you. The longer you fight to avoid the inevitable, the more pain and anguish you cause yourself. Submission is essential here and that, in itself for many of us, is a monumental struggle.

- In order to get to a point in your life where you are comfortable with taking faith-based risks, your faith muscle will need to be exercised. If that sounds easy enough, be warned that this is one of the most painful experiences you will have throughout the process. Faith is the strong belief in something that you cannot see. To build your faith, you will be placed in situations that literally look and feel like a trap with no possible way *out*. In all of your brilliant glory, you will not be able to think, speak, or act your way out of certain situations. You will be forced to remain still and let God show up on your behalf. For those of you who are proactive and impatient, this will be the struggle of a lifetime so be prepared. For those who do not have a strong spiritual connection to God, it will be difficult to trust in a source with which you are unfamiliar.

- A renewed thought life can change the course of your destiny, but first it will require the uprooting of your current mindset. The mindset encompasses all of your beliefs, thoughts and actions. What principles do you believe in? How did your life experiences help to shape those sets of beliefs? Why do you think the way you do? How does that particular type of thinking influence your actions?

For example, your restoration may involve a revelation of the fact that due to past experiences, you have deep-rooted abandonment and trust issues. Certain experiences have led you to believe that people are generally unreliable and untrustworthy. Some of the people closest to you may have abandoned you at a time when they were needed most. As a result, your violated trust will then create an invisible barrier in any future relationships regardless of type. You will subconsciously (or quite intentionally) refrain from any deep level of intimacy within the relationship out of fear. Regardless of how amazing the relationship is progressing, you will secretly be awaiting the day for that person to prove themselves untrustworthy. In this case, your "stinking" thinking will yield if not force the physical manifestation of the negativity permeating your mind. A renewed thought life will require you to come to terms with issues that have been buried in the recesses of your mind. Strap up your boots and prepare for a war between your past and present on the battlefield of your mind. The sanding process will be painful, but incredibly rewarding. When it is complete, you will possess an unprecedented strength that affirms you can achieve just about anything!

The third step in the restoration process is **staining**. It is here that God applies color to what has been stripped and sanded. The 'color' in this case is the restoration of joy, peace, love, and hope. You are being colored and covered by the grace of God, which enables you to press forward and strive toward a better standard of living. The word 'color' itself has so many different meanings. One of which is used to describe someone's character or nature. Have you ever heard someone say, "He/she showed their true colors today." The implication of that statement is to illustrate an unexpected revelation of an individual's true character. During this particular point in the process, God is recoloring the essence of you. Your deep-rooted seeds of anger will be exchanged for happiness. The war that once raged within will be exchanged for peace. The hatred that consumed your heart will be exchanged for love. Fear that has held you captive will be replaced with unwavering faith. Most importantly your pessimism will be exchanged by an optimistic outlook on life. All of the old characteristics that no longer serve you will be gone. Everything about you will be transformed as you will have been stained and colored to reflect the beauty of the almighty God.

YOU ARE BEING COLORED AND COVERED BY THE GRACE OF GOD.

The last step in this process is called **finishing**. It is here that God will apply all of the finishing touches to your life. In the last step, as you were colored the changes started to manifest from the inside out. Many of the changes that took place during that phase were internal attributes. It is during the last portion of the process that you will begin to notice an outward and physical manifestation of the restoration process. When you are fully restored, you will naturally exude light and joy! Your wounds will be completely healed as you prepare yourself to greet the world as a new and improved individual.

EVERYONE AROUND YOU WILL BE ABLE TO SEE GOD'S LOVE ILLUMINATE.

Words often used to help describe this portion of the process include: Developed. Distinguished. Perfected. Experienced. Those are all words that are synonymous with being refined. As you bask in the glow of your newness, you will notice a shift in your walk, talk, and mindset as pertaining to you. You will no longer neglect what matter most. Your dreams and aspirations will become non-negotiable and you will stop at nothing to actualize them. You will unapologetically let your inner light shine because you know with utmost certainty who and how valuable you are to God's kingdom. You will have clear definition of what you want versus what you don't want. You will hold all members of your inner and outer circle accountable for their actions because you now know the importance of mutually beneficial relationships. Most importantly, you will be ready for love again. But not "love" as the unhealthy, self-destructive and emotional imprisonment it once was. You will be ready for the type of love that God has created just for you. Ironically enough, be prepared for the love of your life to come at a time when you least expect it, but are most ready and prepared to receive it. Although difficult, this process will position you perfectly atop a pinnacle of mental, physical, and spiritual health. Rising above all of the adversity, you will delight in an aerial view of the life you want for yourself and full access to the tools necessary to create it!

Life as you know it will change because you are a completely different person both inside and out. All who had counted you out will be astonished by the 'new and improved' you. Until now, you've heard many people use the phrase "blessed and highly favored" but by the end of the restoration process you will know for yourself exactly what those words mean. You will have everything you need within to live an amazing life. You will consistently wear the full armor of God and therefore are no longer susceptible to the snares of the enemy. This is not to say you will never be tempted to stray away from what God has intended for you. However, now you will have the gift of discernment and be able to make decisions based on the counsel of your spirit. Your definition of love now matches God's definition and that makes you *ready* to experience the kind of love God intended for you.

The restoration process is difficult and that is precisely why it is avoided by so many. Immediately after a break-up, some people are so broken that they immediately seek to replace the individual and fill the void of being lonely. At their lowest point they may exhibit neediness, dependency, fearfulness, and require validation of worth from other people. In this state, these types of people unfortunately do not have clear self-definition and as a result, define themselves by their ability to maintain relationships even if it is with people who do not genuinely love them. Others are enslaved to confusion and although their relationships are loveless, they are unable to genuinely identify the deficiency. The reason is because they have not yet learned the *true* definition of love. The only way to know love is to know God. GOD IS LOVE.

Take the time to give God the glory for being an ever-present help to you during your restoration process. Immediately thereafter, find yourself a mirror and thank the person you see in the reflection. You've done the hard work. You've put in the time necessary to be successful. You've seen the process through to completion and now you are free from the emotional bondage that has kept you from realizing your greatness and receiving the right relationship God intended for you. Let each passing day be a reminder of how blessed you are to have new opportunities to laugh, learn and love.

Go forward in faith as a new man or woman in Christ --
renewed, refreshed, and **RESTORED**.

ABOUT THE AUTHOR

DOROTHY WARD is a transformational author, motivational speaker, and life coach. She intentionally uses her gift of writing to edify and motivate her readers.

Years of emotional turmoil experienced after a failed relationship was the genesis of Dorothy's latest project, "Restoration: A Transformational Journey after Heartbreak". She believes her work will inspire both Christian men and women to reclaim their lives following the emotional setback of an ended relationship. This book explores heartbreak from a different perspective as it acknowledges the emotional space of the reader while requiring authenticity and accountability. Dorothy empowers the reader with insight that facilitates the future development of healthier, interdependent, and mutually beneficial relationships. Most importantly, Dorothy helps the reader develop a better relationship with themselves and God the Creator.

Dorothy currently resides in New Jersey and enjoys spending quality time with family, friends and traveling.

END NOTES

toxic. 2014. In *Merriam-Webster.com*. Retrieved May 8, 2014, from http://www.merriam-webster.com/dictionary/toxic

soul. 2014. In *Merriam-Webster.com*. Retrieved May 8, 2014, from http://www.merriam-webster.com/dictionary/soul

Baird, Derik E. (May 2009). Neilson: Americans Watching More TV Than Ever; Web and Mobile Video Up too. Retrieved from http://www.debaird.net/blendededunet/2009/05/nielsen-americans-watching-more-tv-than-ever-web-and-mobile-video-up-too.html

Salovey, P. & Mayer, J.D. (1990). Emotional intelligence. *Imagination, Cognition, and Personality*, Vol. 9, 185-211.

Goleman, D. (1995). *Emotional Intelligence*. New York: Bantam.

Goleman D. (1998). *Working with Emotional Intelligence*. New York: Bantam.

Petrides, K.V., Furnham, A. & Mavrovelli, S. (2007). Trait Emotional Intelligence: Moving Forward in the Field of EI. *Social Development*, Aug 2007, Vol. 1(3) 537-547.

Darwin, C. (1965). *The expression of the emotions in man and animals.*(Rev. ed). Chicago: The University of Chicago Press. (Original work published 1872).

Hochschild, A. R. (1983). *The managed heart: Commercialization of human feeling.* Berkeley: University of California Press.

Seyle, H. (1956). The Stress of Life. New York: McGraw-Hill.

www.ingramcontent.com/pod-product-compliance
Lightning Source LLC
Chambersburg PA
CBHW021230090426
42740CB00006B/469